zerodrifter

Thomas Kling

zerodrifter
selected poems 1983-2005

*translated from German
by Andrew Duncan*

Shearsman Books

First published in the United Kingdom in 2019 by
Shearsman Books
50 Westons Hill Drive
Emersons Green
BRISTOL
BS16 7DF

Shearsman Books Ltd Registered Office
30–31 St. James Place, Mangotsfield, Bristol BS16 9JB
(this address not for correspondence)

www.shearsman.com

ISBN 978-1-84861-656-1

Acknowledgements
Some of the translations here were previously published in
Chicago Review; Depart, Kaspar; krakel-kakel-ugn.

The translation of this work was supported
by a grant given by the Goethe-Institut, London.

Contents

4. from *nacht.sicht.gerät.*

5. from *morsch*

6. from *Fernhandel*

7. from *Sondagen*

8. from *Auswertung der Flugdaten*

96 glints in 96 eyes

Andrew Duncan

Thomas Kling (1957-2005) published successively the volumes *testing of heart-strengthening remedies, flavour enhancer, fuel rods, rotting, night. vision.equipment, Long-distance Trade, Soundings, Evaluation of Flight Data*. His collected poems run to 975 pages. He rarely used capital letters, a trait he said referred back to Stefan George, another poet from Kling's home town of Bingen. Kling went to school not far away, in Düsseldorf.

A quick look at the indigenous *Rezeption* of Kling reveals keywords such as, *on the boundary between oral and literary; speech archaeology; speech installation; polyphony; performance-oriented; punk; velocity; media freak; slang, street talk; topography of cities*. But most of the commentators have talked about virtuosity, how you can isolate the elements of poetic creation which are difficult and how Kling outstrips all the competition in just those aspects. The polyphony mentioned is his vocal ability to differentiate, rhythmically and tonally, different voices running like strips through the texture of the poem, and how the rapid jump-cuts of the verbal text are saved from chaos by this differentiation and also act as a foil to exhibit it to perfection. When Kling wrote a ten-page sequence about bird song (*vogelherd. microbucolika*) there was a latent self-reference to himself as someone who could sing like a bird and, undoubtedly, utter vocal lines that imitated all those birds. Perhaps no other poet has had that stunning combination of hypervivid visual sensibility and hypervivid acoustic sensitivity to all aspects of the verbal sign.

As this would imply, translating Kling is like diving from a church steeple. Success seems the least likely outcome. What do I know about his style, after spending so long feeling along it, syllable by syllable? That it represents a version of the sublime based in hypersensitivity and a silencing of the self to reach pure receptivity. That it is reactive to an amazing frequency width of signals from the outside world, from zenith to pupil. That it is unlike anyone else. Nonstandard spellings – often transcriptions of Rhineland dialect or pronunciation – are a regular feature of Kling's work. I have not reproduced this because the effect in English is displeasing. I am not sure why but the implication of slang in English is overwhelmingly casual and negligent, whereas Kling's poems demand acuity all the time.

One place to start is with a horizon of around 1977 and a musical style: punk, very popular in Düsseldorf and having its headquarters there in the Ratinger Hof, a club/bar to which Kling dedicated three 'documentaries'. Technically, this implied a style of speed, with endless rapid cuts and short snatches, surely composed into larger wholes but at first unmediated and stripped of an interpretative voice-layer. 'Zero drifter' is a kind of translation of '-zerhacker', (in the first line of 'Ratinger Hof zb 2'), a key word because it is so complicated in meaning. The basic meaning is 'chop to bits' which is a reference to dancing because it also contains the word *Hacke*, heel. So it's about punk dancing, inimical to floors. But 'zerhacker' is also an electronics term for a device which chops up a signal as a way of stabilising it against brief fluctuations. It is used for example in "zero drift" amplifiers and especially in car radios. This archaeology of words is typical for Kling. Because we are in a club in the throes of a rock gig, amplifiers are quite important. We are in the product placement region of Little Richard talking about a "solid sender": e.g. "My Marlinda/ she's a solid sender/ you'd better surrender." The idea of cutting a signal up into a million segments too brief to be consciously heard is a sly reference to Kling's style: blurring speed, endless cuts, then unity at a higher level. A picture in a fly's eye. After the hacking up the poem is integral, not a frass of fragments. So I ended up with *zerodrifter* as the overall title. (Punk as in crumbling wood fit for tinder could be translated as *morsch*, the title of Kling's 1996 book.) There is a selected poems of Kling in Germany called *skull magic*, which I didn't like as a title.

Kling preferred the word *sprachinstallation* (speech-installation) to 'performance'. Perhaps this drew attention to the predominance of sound, perhaps it was because 'performance' had rather degraded implications. He keeps using the English word *Sound*. This is more specific than the English source: it flows out of contexts like "the Mersey Sound", like "Look" (the look of a film) it means something recognisable, a feature cluster that moderates a variety of signals and repeats itself. A dandyish word, it ends up as theme song or actually product recognition. The key to short sharp phrases is to catch the call-signs of scenes and experiences, the clusters we use in a kind of neurological trick to orient ourselves in the thousand plains of culture. There are some tunes we want to hear again.

Politically, punk meant not fungus-softened dead wood but a strong reaction against the existing dominant poetic style of new subjectivity (*Neue Subjektivität*) as well as unnervingly fast time signatures. In one remark Kling said that no German poetry between 1965 and 1980 had brought any progress in technique. A wipe-out. Grandiose perhaps but encapsulating the revolt with which our poet began. A combination of hypersensitivity and aggression would be a turn-off. Kling actually did express some aggression towards this generation, accusing them of sentimentality, smugness, and woefully run-down poetic technique. (Austrian poets were excepted from this write-off, aimed at the Federal Republic. I don't think the Democratic Republic featured much in Kling's thinking. Priessnitz and Brinkmann were the '60s poets he excepted from his lament.)

Kling identified *Mediatisierung* (something like *the condition native to media freaks*) as the main new factor arriving in the late Sixties. Poetry is made of information and the universal availability of information, the data discount supermarket, changed the rules for poets. Punk was a dandyish pose and drew that pose in everyday dress from a dedication to media experience which went further than anyone had yet imagined. The 'expert' in the culture of the Republic must now spend time watching clips of rock bands on YouTube and have some grasp of what the Düsseldorf punk scene was. I suspect that the New Subjectivity wave had recognised, in the wake of McLuhan, the power of media products to create a community between consumers, and had explored a passive extension of that community (based to a great extent on rock records and American films) in a way which led the poem itself to atrophy. If you both listen to the same Joni Mitchell album, or both have the same personal reaction when watching TV news, that is a bond. The sharing is implicit and does not need much verbal information to be passed. The poets of that wave don't have a place in the history of poetic style because they had dropped technique out of the poem. The next step was to drop the poem altogether and simply be media voices as DJs on the radio, columnists in newspapers, etc., affirming bonds with people exactly their age but not bothering with the mechanics of writing a poem.

The demo was actually the home of youth culture for a few years, the public space to which poems referred back. The poems were committed (or ideologically debt-laden?), swimming on a big, woolly, youth-culture-togetherness feel in which they had a notably passive and derivative role. Demos march away and collective feels move on. For people Kling's age – and mine – it was obvious around 1976 that the hippy/1968 promise was not going to be kept and that the future had to be rethought from the ground up. For Kling, that meant rejecting the ideal of dropping out and getting with a work ethic and command of technology.

Transition to a new and shining world of endless data meant the end of conventional ethics – the obsolescence of a finite set of literary playing-cards as the basis for poems which cycled through an equally finite set of positions. Kling was not writing poems about the government. You can't write about interactions in the world in a form language so many times poorer than the formal range of the world. Poetry had to go through complexity to come back with anything meaningful about justice and rights. The protest generation closed the gap between youth culture and 'poetry' and our poet stuck with youth culture but redesigned the new poem so that it was data-rich and no longer dumbed-down to meet an anti-verbal generation. Reliance on photos was the medium for this: people were used to abundant information presented as photos and moving pictures. Kling is supremely an "audio-visual" poet. His books from DuMont included CDs in the package.

The need to be a Nice Person and so to deliver Nice Words means that you can't depict human self-interest, rapacity, tendency to dominate. As these are the axes on which most human situations are constructed, this inhibition excludes you from describing almost any human situation tellingly and vividly. Any writer who gets tired of this and returns to descriptive writing is going to be accused of damaging a beautiful ideal. Most idealists are guilty of self-idealisation – not least in Germany. A certain earnest lyricism of the mid-century was a remake of religious discourse with its abstraction, its vagueness, its regression, its apparent generosity. It was due to fade from view a few minutes after religious discourse faded from view: double parallel downward curves. Modernity had a new pulse train. Kling did not set himself out as a person nicer than everyone else.

That 'new subjectivity' is not a familiar concept to English readers because it was not of export quality. It seems to be inevitable that, when a literary style has reached final conclusions and terminal exhaustion, young poets should be immersed in it and react with passionate negativity; and that the people whose cultural assets are poems written in that style should by then have become editors, members of prize panels, professors, etc., and be in a position to be shocked by the impiety of the young. But meanwhile there was a generation that no longer wanted to be guardians of ethics.

Short units of sense generally mean a shallow attention, the flight of awareness constantly emptying out and sinking back to null. Rapid cuts start to work if they relate to a larger whole, a vortex, which is exciting from whatever point we look at it. Then, cuts do not empty the attention flight but leave it floating, growing. Kling's ability to compose by a rattle of edits works only after a preliminary hunt for a subject which will engulf the eye as we look at it. He found his vortices, objects whose anatomy justified the flock of brief snatches and allowed spiralling cumulative effects, restless shifts of angle, serial climaxes. Kling's choice of subjects is one of the richest of any modern poet.

"Petersburger hängun'" is another favourite theme for Kling, a phrase that refers to the way pictures were hung in a certain imperial palace, crowded and jammed up against each other, jostling for space. The poet uses this phrase to describe his portraits of cities. Again the quality of small units in large numbers jammed into a frame and forced to interact with each other is attractive to the poet. Flicker pictures. He likes the over-stimulation of so many channels of data and likes spatial order to be disrupted so that he can pick a route of his own. This is a visual aesthetic, he doesn't like emptiness, white spaces, reverence and the installation of sensory deprivation as the basis for elevated responses. The montages of super-vivid flashes to evoke cities (Vienna, Manhattan, etc.) are breathless. The footloose effect may be typical of the domestic image diet in an era of internet PC screens and digital files. Kling's immersion in this new landscape is a way of surrendering and winning, scoring as the top consumer in a new consumption land.

Critics speak of the absence of a lyrical I, a Me-poem. We have direct recording of sensation rather than having the "I" word frame the sensations (as assets? as owned things? as outpourings?). While I think an intense sensibility is basic to most of these poems, I concede that the word "I" and its relatives hardly ever appear in them. That hardly means that beauty has been exiled from this new form of poetry, that it has no room for the exquisite, the sublime, for landscapes and birdsong. Rather than reproducing a personality (as a religio-cultural asset, like an old church), Kling's work reproduces a state of desire, an optical craving. (The word *I* does appear in the poem about Walter Serner, which flashes back to the poet visiting Karlsbad with his mother aged 15.) It is not the pristine self which is authentic, but the poem.

Like the art historian Horst Bredekamp, who deals with the gestural language of politicians on TV side by side with the products of Renaissance portraiture, Kling has a boundless visual diet. He deals with TV as well as with paintings and, often, postcards or old photographs from the magnificent collections of museums. Whatever is a visual artefact partakes of the same language. So many of his poems are based on visual experiences (there is no "I" in a photograph). 'Retina scans' could sum them up – but his is not a passive engagement. Look at 'Larven', where he is literally looking at a photo of Papuans, dating from Germany's era as a hopeful colonial empire, but the poem is much more about the pre-suppositions of the photographer and about the marketing which creates expectations among the intended audience and so structures the visual experience. Kling doesn't think you can look at a photo of Melanesians and get unmediated access to their souls. The surface of the photograph is a mirror which the unconscious views of the persons looking at it fill, and overflow the visual space.

We are dealing with a very rare ability to project oneself into external masses or skies of data, winged and disembodied like an angel, lifted by light. That very pure ability to lose yourself in passing over into what is forever alien, to know its defiant complexity, to flow into its patterns. With bat-like powers, sucking in the sky through one's fingers, diving on loops of sound. Typical for our poet is the use of words from the technical language of TV directing and photography. Take the word "Strecke", for example (used in the poem translated as 'Black Forest 1932'). The word has several meanings but here is used specifically in the sense of a documentary photographer speaking of a "group" of photos which belong together. In a magazine you would call this a "spread" (*Bilderstrecke*), on the internet you would call it a "gallery" – I have used the word spread.

It may be helpful, if reading about portable bee-boxes, to have walked through a German forest and seen these wooden hives, moved into the woods so the bees can tuck into the local specialities. English bees, like English poets, prefer to stay at home. As Kling grabs information from images, there is the possibility of returning to the ancestral visual, the source. This brings the game to an end. You can't flip the poem back to the photograph without a regression. Clearly you could collect a hundred or so photographs and create a sort of Kling-gallery. This would lose the transformation, the retina scan track. The third 'data object' is the pattern which the reader constructs in reaction to the poem, pursuing its original integrity and strangeness. Kling's eye is sensitive to the tiniest flecks of dust and however far you pursue its courses there are always more details to recover. An available commentary on Kling's Vienna poems recovers endless details which would surely elude someone who had not lived in Vienna. The documentary density yields us the security of a deep complex, stabilised by its multiple attachments to a reality which in the end saves us from mere melancholy. He sees something we don't. Very well. The photographs may help.

The reception also records a transition with the First World War poems (in *Fernhandel*, 1999) from punk to a more deliberate and less intense style, with many pastoral and archaeological themes. It's hard to be angry over 40. The pace becomes more largo. More space is made for calm and long-period events. This allowed some of the most characteristic, unexpected, and profound works of our poet.

It is hard to explain why Kling has line ends splitting syllables. The effect seems to be a rapid tempo of some music already running which the poem is caught up in: where the poet doesn't react quickly enough the line end jumps in and breaks the syllable. The same is true of repeated definite articles, the stuttering effect is like someone dealing with music going too fast for him. This effect was alienating but belonged with the soundtrack of punk in the clubs, the permanently breathless tempo. It is documentary in its way.

Critics have picked up on the tag "gedicht ist ahnenstrecke" (in 'schwarzwald 1932' and meaning "poem is a spread of ancestors") in order to explore a personal mythology of German-language poetry to which Kling connected himself. We would start with Friederike Mayröcker, whose method of acquiring large numbers of short snatches of language fragments and sequencing them into larger poetic wholes leads directly to Kling. The psychological atmosphere of Kling is completely different, but the link is there. Kling's stay in Vienna (associated also with the poets Artmann, Jandl, Priessnitz) in 1979-80 was very important to his imagination of a style and subsequent technical development to the stage of being able to write poems in that style. More widely, Kling created a "spread of ancestors" for himself, as laid out in the selections of his *Sprachspeicher*, a revisionist work which is comparable to Mon and Heissenbüttel's 1973 *anti-anthologie*. Figures like Oswald von Wolkenstein, Walter Serner, and Rudolf Borchhardt now seem to be visible through Kling's eyes, more than in any other way. Maybe Austria didn't have the American influence that West Germany underwent, and this was the key to a much more adequate reaction to the primal modernist landscape, uncovered after the effective blanking-out by National Socialism.

I published a pamphlet of Kling translations in 1996. This was based on his selected poems of 1994 and reflected what I immediately responded to. I met him in April 2000 in Cambridge. The second time around I have paid attention to the poems which German commentators were especially interested in, for example the 'Ratinger Hof' poems. These were not poems that I "got" on first reading, but they yielded more in the end. The 'Ratinger Hof' period is where Kling was closest to a collective culture and to everyone else his age. He almost never used youth-cult slang although there is the odd term like *flug* (a line, a hit) soaked up as a kind of sonic documentary. Translating slang from thirty years ago really would be a lost cause. I translated more poems in 2000 for a *Chicago Review* special issue on New German Writing and a whole lot in 2015.

I can't remember who gave me copies of the special issues of *Schreibheft* and *text + kritik* on Kling but I am very grateful, they were indispensable.

ANDREW DUNCAN
January 2019

ratinger hof, zb 1

für juliette

hände die nach reis fiebern,
nach – kontinentwechsel – reiß
verschlüssn; tablettenhände,
säure »ICH KANN NACHTS«
im -gedrängel wächst meine hand
ums glas, wächst später um ihre
schulter; ihre neunzehnjährige
schalter wächst mir entgegn; »ICH
KANN NACHTS NICHT« zähne kappen
mein sehnerv, das schwappt alles
gegen mein lederpanzerung, gegenseh-
nerv, gegen ihre nackte schulter,
gegen die zähne der reißverschlüsse
»MEER«: das insektengedrängel;
aus wespenhälsen schwappts stich
wort aufs stichwort, schwappts
gestichel, stechn »SCHLAFN« das
gestochne:
      LASS DIE SATZSTANZE STANZN/
DIREKT DAS CHINESISCHE HOROSKOP/SCHICK
MIR DEIN HOPI TELEGRAMM/ICH GEB DIR
DIE WORTGAROTTE DASS DU SIE ANMIR
AUSPROBIERN KANNZ/, "GÄNSEFÜSSCHEN"/ICH
KANN OHNE DAS WORT PRRSHNG NICHT LEHM/
LADI SATTSCHTNZE TNZN ich spür ihre
schönschwarzn fühler ich will mein
schöngelbes loswern ich geb ihrs
stichwort

ratinger hof, documentary report 1

for juliette

hands that crave for rice,
for – shift of continents – zip
fasteners: pill hands,
acid   "I AM AVAILABLE NIGHTS"
in the crush my hand grows
around the glass, later around her
shoulder; her 19 year old on-off
switch grows towards me; "I AM NOT
AVAILABLE NIGHTS" teeth snip
my optic nerve, it all splashes up
against my leather armour, counter optic
nerve, against her naked shoulder,
against the teeth of the zips
"SEA": the insect crush;
out of the throats of wasps splashes slogan
on slogan, splashes the
sting, stab "SLEEP" the
sharpened:
        LET THE PRINT STAMPER STAMP/
RIGHT AWAY THE CHINESE HOROSCOPE/ SEND
ME YOUR HOPI TELEGRAM/ I'LL GIVE YOU
THE WORD GAROTTE SO YOU CAN TRY
IT OUT ON ME/ "QUOTE MARKS"/ I
CANT LIVE WITHOUT THE WORD PRRSHNG
LEDDA PRISTAMPER TMP I feel her
beautifully black antennae I want to get
rid of my beautifully yellow one I give her the
slogan

ratinger hof, zb 2

wenn das die fraumutter wüßt das
herzimleib tät ihr zrspringn

UNTERM -ZERHACKER das schuhe zertanzn;
sorgfältig epilierte wadn vor den boxn
bockbierflaschn; das das zerhackn;
mitteilung aus dragée pupillen, -häute,
dezibelschübe; verunglückte mitteilung
durch milchglas, naja, durch trennscheiben
halt; reißende iris, rasierte muschi,
dezibelschübe, das lichtzerhackn die die
zertanzer in ihren »stiefel-muß-sterm«-
stiefeln
      wälzer heißt pogo! vulkan fiber
wieder PVC! merkts euch! ihr säcke mit
den verrutschten kathetern mit den ein
gewachsnen unlackierten mit den den
nägeln an zehen an spitzfüßn an bettlägrigen
innen drin in altnkranknheim
                    (achso mit-
teilung durchtrennscheiben – nichts mehr
aus dragéepupilln aus tablettenhand aus
pferchhäutn aus mehligem zahnfleisch hinter
infarktlippn; doch eins noch ihr verd
verdun ihr verdunblick ende der durch
sage) dezibelschübe, gezupfte brauen,
unter der der lichthacke das das zertanzn
IM DRITTN STADIUM FUNKTIONIERT AUCH DIE
ONANIE NICH MEHR DER PATIENT HAT KEIN B
DÜRFNIS NACH GENITALER BETETIGUN DER AN
BLICK DER GERUCH DI E BERÜHRUN DAS ABLE
CKN ODER KÜSSN DES SCHUHES GENÜGN

ratinger Hof, documentary report 2

If your mother only knew that
her heart would burst in her body…

UNDER THE -KICKERTOBITS the dancing your shoes to death;
carefully waxed calves in front of crates
of bock-beer bottles; the the kicking to bits;
bulletin from dragée pupils, -skins,
decibel throbs; crashed bulletin
through milky glass, that's it, through partition
panes; jerking iris, shaved pubis,
decibel throbs, stamping light to bits the the
kicking apart in her "boots must die"
boots;
      waltz is now the pogo! vulcanite
against PVC! get with it! you bags with
the the slipped out catheters with the in
grown unpainted with the the
nails on toes on sharp feet on bedridden
in there in the old people's nursing home
                    (I see informing

through partition panes – nothing more
from dragée pupils from tablet hand from
congested skin from crumbling gums behind
blue lips; but one more thing their verd
verdun their verdun look end of
bulletin) decibel throbs, plucked eyebrows.
under the heel of light the the dancing to bits
IN THE THIRD STAGE EVEN ONANISM NO
LONGER WORKS THE PATIENT HAS NO N
EED FOR GENITAL ACTIVITY A SI
GHT A SMELL A TOUCH OR LIC
KING OR KISSING THE SHOE SUFFICE

ratinger hof, zett beh (3)

»o nacht! ich nahm schon
flugbenzin...«

nachtperformance, leberschäden,
schrille klausur
          HIER KÖNNEN SIE
ANITA BERBER/VALESKA GERT BESICHTIGEN
MEINE HERRN . . KANN ABER INS AUGE GEHN
stimmts outfit? das ist dein auftritt!
schummrige westkurve (»um entscheidende
millimeter geschlagen«)
                    gekeckerte -fetzen
»süße öhrchen«, ohrläppchen metallverschraubt
beschädigtes leder, monturen, blitze
beschläge, fischgrät im parallel-
geschiebe; sich uberschlagendes, -lapp
endes keckern (»gestern dä lappn wech«);
unser sprachfraß echt junkfood, echt
verderbliche ware; süße öhrchen, wir
stülpen unsere mäuler um JETZT mit der
(kühlschrank)nase flügeln (yachtinstinkt,
(»paar lines gezogn«); nebenbei erklärter
maßen blitzkrieg/blickfick (JETZT LÄC
HELN!); havarierte augenpaare (schwer
geädert), »man sieht sich«, kiesel im
geschiebe, man sieht nichts aber: über
gabe/rüberreichen von telefonnummern
(JETZT LECKEN!)
DAS HAARREGISTER: bei
steiler fülle, grannig gestylt, hoch
gesprühter edelwust, fiftyfifty
gesperberte fönung, cherokeegerädert,
barbieverpuppung, teddysteiff, »sekthell
ihr busch«, weekend-allonge, Yves-Klein-blau,
pechschwanz, schläfenraster, freigelegte
schädeldecke, »um entscheidende millimeter
geschlagen!«

Ratinger Hof, documentary report 3

*"o night! I have already taken
on flying fuel…"*

night performance, liver damage,
shrill study hour
          HERE YOU CAN VIEW
ANITA BERBER/ VALESKA GERT
GENTLEMEN . . BUT CAN TURN OUT BADLY
is the outfit right? this is a show!
twilight west stand ("beaten by the
crucial millimetres")
                     ranting -snatches
"sweet little ears", earlobes screwed with metal
damaged leather, regalia, lightning
studs, fishbones in parallel-
thrust; overrunning, -lapping
ranting ("got my licence confiscated yesterday");
our speech-meals total junk food, total
corruption goods; "sweet little ears", we
turn our mouths inside out NOW with the
(refrigerator)nose wings (yacht instinct,
"snorted a few lines"); incidental openly
declared blitzkrieg eyefuck ("NOW
SMILE!"); wrecked pairs of eyes (heavily
veined), "be seeing you", gravel in
the motor, you don't see anything but: hand
over, reaching over of telephone numbers
(NOW LICK!)
THE DIRECTORY OF HAIR; in
steep fullness, styled like awns of wheat, sprayed
high noble disarray, two-toned,
hawk-like hairdrying, a Cherokee wheel,
in a Barbie cocoon, teddybear stiff, "light as
champagne her sheaf", weekend-extension, Yves-Klein blue,
tar ponytail, pattern on temples, exposed
skullcap, "beaten by crucial
millimetres!"

(von der kette
gelassen; bereit, zeitig, zum sprung;
zum absprung bereit, die jungens: paar
kanaken plattmachn, gefletschte pupillen,
panzerglasig; vollgestopft mit guten
pillen werden sie dann unter vorrückende
tanks gejagt, »haste ma ne mark für taxi«);
gerädert, bei steiler fülle, OP-bläue,
pechschwanz, schädelraster, ums ganze
haarregister laberschäden; sicherheit ja
die einzige ja: UM FÜNF WIRD HIER
DAS LICHT ANGEHN . . DAS VOLLE LICHT . .
AUFTRITT VON PHANTOMSCHMERZEN . . UND
ANGST DAS KALTE LAKEN

(let off the leash;
ready, on the moment, for the jump;
ready for the launch, the lads: bashing a
few Kanaks flat, pupils bared,
like armoured glass; stuffed full of good
pills they are then chased under advancing
tanks, "you got a Deutschmark for a taxi");
dead with fatigue, completely tanked up,
operating theatre blue tinge,
tar ponytail, skull pattern; around the whole
hair directory blabber damage; security is
the main thing isn't it: AT FIVE THE LIGHT
WILL GO ON ... UNMITIGATED LIGHT ...
ARRIVAL OF PHANTOM PAINS ... AND
FEAR THE COLD SHEET

käptn brehms verklappung
(seestück)

sag an lies ab deine richterskala
sack ab nimm die kurve die fieber
kurve verklapp sie; sei schlaf;
sei rochen zitter aal mit den augen
durch die der tag geht der tang; sei
schlafkrankheit; käptn brehm schreit
auf schreckt aus mangrovesümpfen
(aaltraum die tsetse) fliege auf der
schulter; sein ins-meer-finger sticht
zu: käptn b verklappt sein zeige
finger bei hochgrad Celsius verklappt
sein auflagenstärke sein faunaraum;
muß tierchen abhaken immerzu; zusehends
sein brehm wirdundwird schmaler; seine
alben seine elben (tunnel) mit (bäuch –
lings) geschwulst müßn verklappt wern;
DIE BERICHTE: vom schneebrett lostretn
(liane vulgo lawine); küstendienst
straßenzustand (»auf der a 3 kommts
ihnen«); weg- und wetterwarten; beobachtung
von homunculus stratokumulus undsofort;
der käptn verklappt sich: den klima
schalter umgelegt krächzend mit ver
eintem krächzn.

captain brehm's offshore effluent
(a marine piece)

call out read off your richter scale
sag down take the curve the fever
curve sluice it; be sleep;
be ray electric eel with the eyes
through which the day goes the seaweed; be
sleeping sickness; captain brehm cries
out starts up from mangrove swamps
(eel dream the tsetse) fly on his
shoulder; his into-the-sea finger jabs
in: captain b sluices his index
finger at high-point celsius sluices
his print run his fauna realm;
has to unhook tiny animals all the time; visibly
his brehm grows smallerandsmaller; his
albums his elbes (tunnel) with (belly
down) overgrowth must be sluiced;
THE REPORTS: step off the snowdam
(liana found in avalianche); coast guarding
state of the street; ("it's coming your way
along the a3"); path- and weather-watches; observation
of stratocumulus homunculus and so on;
the captain sluices himself into the sea: the air
conditioning turned round croaking with
a creak in time.

hermesbaby, auspizium

gezüngelte liebkosung,
erstlingsgabe deine ernsten licht-
beschriftungen;
        gespeichert;
angelehntes styropor (wandtafeln):
gespickte auffangbecken, künftige
reservoire; staksschritt durchs
zimmer, belagerter bösendorfer;
oder, den mantel geschultert,
im café museum; deine scheuende stimme
die (bären?)franse erreicht deine braue;
durchs zimmer jagen die schwalben
unausgesetzt ihr winkliges rufen,
hakenschlagend, und sorgsame
kurskorrektur wer
will das voraussehen?
        solch erkämpftes
trinkwasser, (vogel)perspektiven
umgekehrte kontinentdrift, offene
herzadresse und -schwall!
        beschriftetes
licht deine ungezügelten sprachen!

(für Friederike Mayröcker)

hermesbaby, auspicium

tongue flickering caress,
first fruits your serious light
-onscriptions;
                    stored registers;
leaning styrofoam (wall boards):
crib tags drainage basins, future
reservoirs; big strides through
the room, besieged Bösendorfer;
or, coat on your shoulders,
in the museum café: your shying voice,
the (bear's?) fringe down to your eyebrows;
through the room the swallows chase
without pausing their zigzag cry,
feinting, and careful
correction of course who
wants to foresee that?
                    such fought-for
drinking water, (bird's eye) perspectives,
reverse continental drift, public
heart-address and -surge!
                    written-on
light your unbridled languages!

(for Friederike Mayröcker)

direktleitung

tritte gegn die -flügel gegn
gerangelte wühltische, ein
von-der-kette-gelassn!, unsägliches
drehtür-vaudeville und nicht sagbare
absagbare mühlenauftritte; fütterung
der raubtiere: am gerüst primatn-
gehangel, sumsemänner krabbeln, im
lakngewühl ein stallgerammel unwieder
bringliches insektnsystem oder kluge
witterung der wanderratte;
               gerüstet; aufm
bau aufm turm die sprachpoliere (siehe unten,
kelle hoch) laute schlagend, lauteschl
agend zur rapunzelstund, belinste luke und
abgestiegen zur siebtn sohle: kienspan tropf
stein augnklapp; auf blutgerüstn, vorne
wird tapfer gestrickt, weiterhin das schwuppdi
wupp: kopf losgewordn, stückwerk hingekegelt
(»wirklich, ganze arbeit«);
               gerüstet, wander-
stäbe für alle; hinter den stäbn in den
etagn im betoniertn granit: das flipperge-
flackert (»fink wie leder«, »leda an schwan
auf stahlfrequenz«, »zäh, windhund & fleißig:
kommen«, »plan 3, anruf genügt«), das auffla
ckern und auslöschn strohbässe fisteltenöre
feierliches kastratntum im bunkerchor, on stage
walkürensounds zischender prothesn: SCHON ACHZICH-
TAUSEND VORSTELLUN'! UNSRE BELIEBTE KONVENTION
ELLE NAPALM-OPERETTE! INCLUDING VÖLKERJACKPOT!
(»dochdoch, ganze arbeit«);

(»treffliche cs-granate«)
             im ruhe zustand die
schattnmodelle voll goldammerscheiße
schattnmorellen die augn, zugefiedeltes

direct transmission

kicks against the pianos, against
tangled rummage tables, a
letting off the chain!, unspeakable
revolving-door vaudeville and unmentionable
negotiable treadmill-showtimes; feeding
of predators: on the scaffolding clustering
primates, beetles scrabble for a lost leg, in the
rumpled sheets a stall thronging unrep
eatable insect system or clever
whiffing of the wandering rat;
                                 equipped; on the
site on the tower the babel frontmen (see below,
trowel high) twang their lute, twang
that thing at Rapunzel time, gaze lifted to roof window and
descent to the seventh basement: pine flares stalac
tite blinker; on gibbet staging, in front
they are cheerfully knitting, further off the whee
here we go: less by a head, piecework like a ninepin,
("really, a noble effort");
                                 equipped, walking-
staves for all; behind the bars on the levels
in the cemented granite: the pinball-
flashing ("fink as in leather chairs", "leda to the
swan at steel frequency", "tough, greyhound and diligent:
come", "plan 3, the call is enough"), the flick-
ering up and quenching straw manly basses reedy tenors
ritual castrateria in the bunker choir, on the boards
valkyrie effects of hissing dentures: ALREADY EIGHTY
THOUSAND PERFORMANCES! OUR BELOVED CONVENTION
-AL NAPALM OPERETTA! FEATURING GENOJACKPOT!
("yes yes, a noble effort");

("brilliant CS grenades")
                                 in retirement the
modelling shadows; full of goldfinch shit
the eyes morello cherries, fiddled shut

heupferdohr, vom krausn mündchen quatscht
die entngrütze so stiefeln dichterzombies
bei neumond dreimal um den erlenbaum und
bis-zum-kotz-dich-aus das teufelsmoor
durchmessn; rührendrührendrührend pflatscht
lehmannscher kompott in rilkes einmachgläser; ja
ja, äpfel-im-schlafrock (handpoliert), schönge
strähntes sprachelchen im geibel-quast oh
geschlummerte inkontinenz im schnucknland, mil
dere leichnkosmetik VERKEHRSKONTROLLE DÜRFNWAMA /
SIE HAM KEIN PROFIL DRAUF/TUT MIR LEID und wei
ter ruhezustand, gedehnter lorbeer, schnabel
tassn UNSER PARLIERMEISTER EMPFIEHLT; auch
den kuckucksuhrn & herrgottschnitzern von das
kritik kräftich auf die hohlen nüsse; im ü
brign gilt (die tatn untn, s.o.): pralinenmeisterin,
zeig dein kandiertn schoß!

the grasshopper ear, from the crooked mouth burbles
the duck gruel so at new moon the poet-
zombies stump three times round the alder and
quarter Grim's Moor to the point
of nausea; stirring stirring stirring spatters
lehmann compote in rilke's preserve jars; yes
yes, coddled in dumplings (hand polished), art-
coiffured burble in a tasselled cap oh
unconscious incontinence in the land of Nod, mild
-er corpse cosmetics TRAFFIC POLICE MAY WE JUST /
YOUR IMAGE ISN'T VISIBLE / SORRY ABOUT THAT and fur
ther retirement, diluted laurel, non dribble
beakers OUR BABEL FRONTMAN RECOMMENDS: the
cuckoo clocks and crucifix whittlers mightily
by the critics on emptied nuts; else-
where applies (the deeds below, *see above*): mistress of the pralines,
show us your candied pubis!

terraingewinne

bespritzte tapisserie, arabeske mit
einschusslöchern, kehren wirs untern
teppich:
             querschnitt (lähmung, aphasie
vom kopf abwärts), offenlegung einer
geduckten häuserzeile, eines druckreifen
viertels in SAGEN WIR beirut;
die verkrustete strähne isfahan
(rotgesoffne gaze), und SAGEN WIR RUHIG
bagdad, trepanierter schädel (grauer
verband, halb übers lid gerutscht:
übergriffe, operative eingriffe an
unseren unbetäubten, bespritzten
leibern SAG KADDISH! bei abnahme
der fensterkreuze, offenbarung ganzer
hauserfronten GUCKKASTENBÜHNE FÜR
ZWANZIG UHR/MEZ
                         rieselung; stockwerke
abgesackt, straßenzüge niedergelegt (wir
sehen bis zum horizont, da gibts immer
neue wölkchen-wölkchen); begutachten wir
das innenleben der mauern: glatt
rasierte stahlträger;
             das gerinnt,
rieselt immerzu; kaftangestalten,
in ihren kehlen, kniekehlen tackern
nähmaschinnadeln: so stochern winselnde
männer im frischen schutt, ein lippen-
loses klageweib hält etwas fest, da;
im laufschritt mörtellunge, erschütterungen:
grad rieselts wieder, maschingewehrnadeln,
das gerinnt;
             ernste kindsmiliz überm
geretteten transistor; ihr minenspiel
bei sportpalastverlautbarungen der
kragenspiegel; kindsmiliz, arabeske

territorial gains

needle-holed tapestry, arabesques with
bullet holes, let's sweep it under
the carpet:
        broken spine (paralysis, aphasia
from the head down), baring of a
crouched row of houses, of a quarter
ready to print in LET'S SAY beirut;
the crusted tress of isfahan
(red-soaked gauzes), and LET'S SAY CALMLY
baghdad, trepanned skull (grey
bandage, slid halfway down over the eye):
infringements, operative interventions on
our unanaesthetised, needled
bodies SAY KADDISH! with the removal
of the windowframes, opening
of whole house fronts FOURTH WALL THEATRE AT
EIGHT/ CENTRAL EUROPEAN TIME
                        trickling down; sagging
stories, flattened parades (we
can see to the horizon, there are ever
renewed cloudy-clouds); let us assess
the inner life of walls: smooth
shaved steel beams;
           it's sifting itself,
trickling all the time; shapes in kaftans,
in their throats, backs of their knees, rattle
sewing machine needles: so whimpering men
jab in the fresh debris, a lipless
wailing-woman has got something, there;
at the double mortar inhalation, concussions:
it's just trickling again, machine-gun needles,
sifting;
      serious child militia over the
rescued transistor; their play of expressions
during the sport palace proclamations of
chevrons; child militia, arabesque

morgenland, ihre geronnene
sandsackkindheit
kehren wir untern teppich;
                    DIE
-ERSTATTUNGSUNTERNEHMER:
                                ungeschlacht:
fotosafari, heia, textsafari ungeschlacht:
»rindenfeld 39 (urnenfeld) zurückerobert«,
»soeben erreicht uns«, »broca unter
beschuß« , »vorgepreschte jeeps, terrain
gewinne«, »unseres nah-korrespondenten
paul broca«, »schuldigen sie die ton
qualität«; virulente einstellungen,
blitzende objektive, diktafone griffbereit,
gezückte belichtungs messer, perfide
fernschreibung GUCKKASTENBÜHNE ZWANZIG
UHR, SAG KADDISH!

orient, their leaking
sandbag childhood, we'll
sweep it under the carpet;
                    THE
REPORT CONTRACTORS:
                         lumpish
photo-safari, huzza, text-safari in lumps:
"cowfield 39 (urnfield) liberated",
"news just in", "broca under
fire", "jeeps dashing forward, gains
of territory", "from our middle-correspondent
paul broca", "logize for the sound
quality"; virulent camera setups,
gleaming lenses, dictaphones handy,
lightmeters drawn, perfidious
telexing FOURTH WALL THEATRE AT
EIGHT, SAY KADDISH!

öffentliche verkehrsmittel

akribischer aufriß, jede menge
handzeichnungen, faustskizzen und
zwar beglaubigte FILM SIE ZUNÄCHST
EINE ÜBE RSICHT (RASIERMESSERTOTALE)
GEHN SIE DANN NÄHER RAN und abgefahren,
das goethesubstrat, regieanwiesung:
hüsteln;
                geduckt, hinter einer ky
rillischen schreibmaschine: ejsenschtejn
nein buñuel;
                »ab
gebrochn!«, »eingedrungen!«; geglittene
badende klinge, sogleich minimalistischer
gong: jedesmal wieder dies hochgeri
ssene tonband!, (am ende abgebissn);
eine durchs taschntuch gesprochene
digitale frau die ihre haltestellen
verkündigt (»gefroren gemacht«); »ausaus-
aus!«, ins bild gerecktes stroheimkinn;
so rushhour drin und draußn dringt in
die köpfe, ballungszentren aufgekratzt;

(»beiseite gesprochn«); FÜHRN SIE SO
DENBE SCHAUER DURCH EINE EINE HALBOTALE
WEITR INDIE SZENE UM deutscher monat,
angeritzt in der verkehrsmitte, deut
licher november, hingestürzte -nacht;

(»bei ungeputzten scheibn«)
-bedeckungen, blindgebliebene hände; auf
gekratzte knallige pärchen, speedpärchen;
angeknallt (»gefroren gemacht, nachts«);
die in miles davis' trompete gebannten
amphetamindandys, ihre in abgestürzter
johannisnacht -belichteten augn DEN
DRÖHNENDEN BLOCKSBERG INSZENIERN WIR

public transport

overworked-over scenario, any quantity
of hand-drawings, sketches by fist and
authenticated too FIRST FILM
AN OVE RVIEW (RAZOR BLADE MEDIUM LONG SHOT)
THEN GO CLOSER TO THEM and driven away,
the goethe substrate, camera directions:
a little cough;
                    stooped, behind a cy-
rillic typewriter: eizenshtein
no buñuel;
          "break
off!", "push in!"; sliding
bathing blade, at once a minimalist
gong: every time this ri-
ding up tape!, (bitten off in the end);
a digital woman speaking
through her handkerchief who announces
her stops ("everybody freeze"); "outout-
out!", a stroheim chin jutting into the frame;
so rush hour out and in drives into
their heads, congestion knots an up mood;

("in an aside"); SO, LEAD THE
SPECTATOR THROUGH A A MEDIUM SHOT
FARTHER INTO THE SETTING german month,
scratched in the middle of the traffic, clear
november, its fallen-down night;

("with dirty panes")
coverings, hands stayed hidden; excited
chic couples, speed couples
turned on ("by the cool night freeze");
the amphetamine dandies bewitched
by miles davis' trumpet, their lit-up eyes in
a fallen-down midsummer night WE'LL ESTABLISH
THE DRONING BLOCKSBERG FROM BIRD'S EYE

AUSSER VOGELPERSPEKTIWE (REINGESCHOBNER
PROSPEKT, KAMERA UNTER STECHAPFEL);
unmittelbar: das hexen im dealerladen;
mit überbelichteten augn freundliche
gebrechliche punx (abgestürzt); am haupt
bahnhof gegrölte ortsangaben, rein-
schüttende fans, anweisung: heraldik und
dosnbier; (ab) JETZT FLIEGN! GLEICH! DILÖCHER
AUSM KESE! (brechn), weisung beiseite:
BESEELTE NATUR!;
                    »sonz nach was?«, «wie
butter einge..« SCHLIESSLICH IN GROSS
AUFNAHME ZEIGN WAS IM EINZELN VORSICH
DEHT
        gebrochene flie
snbläue, halluzinierter meerschaum
schnitt reißverschluß schnitt an offenen
samstagen in heißn bädern die durch
gehend geöffneten pulsadern, gretchens
roter badezusatz ein eingeweichter
anblick HIER KEIN ZITAT! offiziell gegen
nulluhr beglaubigter aufriß, gretchensuppe
unter verschluß; strohs augn (»tief ein
gedrung!«, »knallt rein!«), aus eingestü
rzter perspektive diverse nasnsounds, solch
reinknallender underground, ausm off oheims
stimme: hope you girlies don't hold no hard
feelins 'bout t'nite.

                (für Juliette Tillmanns)

VIEW (SPLICED-IN PERSPECTIVE
SHOT, CAMERA BENEATH THE BELLADONNA);
directly: the chopping and changing in the dealer's pad;
with over-bright eyes friendly
fragile punx (falldown); at the central
station bawled place-names, fans
tipping them back, indication: coats of arms and
canned beer; (off) FLY NOW! RIGHT AWAY! THE HOLES
OUT OF THE CHEESE! (break), direction aside:
SOULFUL NATURE!;
                              "was there anything else?", "like
wrapped butt…" FINALLY IN CLOSE-
UP SHOWING THE DETAILS OF WHAT'S
GOING OON
                    refracted blue
of tiles, hallucination of sea-foam
cut zipper cut on open
saturdays in hot baths the thoroughly
opened wrist veins, gretchen's
red bath salts a pickled
appearance NO QUOTE HERE! sketch
officially attested towards midnight, gretchen soup
under lock; Erich's eyes ("drive
deep in!", "get right in there!"), from tum
bling perspective diverse nasal sounds, such an
underground knockout, "off" stroh's
voice: hope you girlies don't hold no hard
feelins 'bout t'nite…

(for Juliette Tillmanns)

polares piktogramm

> "nicht auszuhalten!"
> *Daniil Charms*

1

    vor der post der apo-
theke (quengelnd köter draußn
angeleint) so laufende motoren auch
von kamin das weiße deutlich weg-
gespreizt;
    rechz daumenkuppe an-
gebrutzelt; mein lieber mann: ich
ganztags ofenheinz!, steh auf
nachts frösteltier, schütt heiß ins
klo, die pseudotatzn an den füßn daß
man in ruhe morgens kackn kann

2

tiefstehendes tageslicht (... schon ab
gesackt); älskling, dein angesägter
schlaf! anschlagendes mein huskieherz, ich
weiß nicht .. ein lichtelch? der durchs
feuer tappt? ist es meine hand die deine
brust so spitz macht?
    gefiepte nacht,
klatschnasse -lippen pidginlippen, im
halbschlaf (vollgekleckert lakn) range-
zognes klammes knie

3

"at kunna arbeta i kyla är
en fråga om koncentration WIE ES UNS
TREIBT!, jag tycker inte at det är
svårt WIE WIRS TREIBEN!, jag studerar
förresten ESKIMÅERNA nu, och de har
det förmodligen ännu kallare GETRIEBN,
ALS DAUNEN-RUSS ZUR DEKKE STEIGEND,
säger thomas kling, düsseldorfbo som
gästar vasa"

polar pictogram

"–unbearable!"
Daniil Kharms

1

       in front of the post office the che-
mist's (whining mongrel outside
on a leash) so running motors also
the enamel clearly split away
from the fireplace;
                right-hand thumb-tip sc-
orched; my dear man!: me
all day stove-hugging!, get up
in the night a shivering creature, pour heat into the
bog, the pseudo-claws on its feet so that
one can cack in peace in the mornings

2

low-lying daylight (...already
sagging); älskling, your sawn-into
sleep! my husky-heart beating up, I don't
know... a light-elk? groping through
the fire? is it my hand which makes
your breast so pointed?
                deer call night,
sopping wet -lips pidgin lips, in
half-sleep (sheets splashed full) drawn up
cold knee

3

"att kunna arbeta i kyla är
en fråga om koncentration AS IT DRIVES US
ON!, jag tycker inte att det är
svårt AS WE GIVE WAY TO IT!, jag studerar
förresten ESKIMÅERNA nu, och de har
det förmodligen ännu kallare DRIFT,
AS DOWN-SOOT RISING TO THE CEILING,
säger thomas kling, dusseldorfbo som
gästar vasa"

4

    (»zur regelung der
outfit-frage«); jetzt wird
das bein verkleidet:
                  bis
übers knie knallgelber alpinistn-
strumpf (ein wollener dragoner), da
rüber socken, schwarze schenkel; halb
schnabelschuh die lappenstiebel (»finn
ischer stalinistn-look der 70er«); aus
unsrer serie: JOSEF KAINZ IN BADEBUXN,
ein absolut gebongter lacherfolg

5

    briefkastn (gestiemt), laufende
motoren, da draußn sind di küsse tief
kühlkost; geschwankt, so kleine dikke
ritter übern burgersteig, verpacktes
blond und hergezeigter atem, schon von
der leine mein gefieptes huskieherz;
arktischer nadeleinsatz: gespickte wange
nasnknistern, die wimpern zugestiemt; ich
krakel KA-KEL-UGN, VED-SPIS, KAMIN, KA-
KEL-UGN
    wo manche kranke mit der karre
übers eis nach schweden brettern.. mensch
schneemensch!, dreissich minus! ich
ganztags ofnheinz

(für Ylva Holländer)

4
    ("on settling the outfit
question"); now the leg
is being disguised:
                 up
to above the knee bursting yellow alpinist-
stocking (a woollen dragoon), over
that socks, black thighs; half
pointed shoe the lappish boots ("finn
ish stalinist-look of the 70s"); from our
range: JOSEF KAINZ IN BATHING TRUNKS,
an absolutely groovy laugh-in

5
    letterbox (snowed-in), running
motors, out there the kisses are deep
freeze delicacies; swaying, such small fat riders
over the pavement, packed
blond and demonstrated breath, my
husky heart already deer-called off the leash;
arctic needle-entrance: ice-pricked cheek
nosecrackling, the eyelashes snowed-up: I
scrawl KA-KEL-UGN, VED-SPIS, FIREPLACE, KA-
KEL-UGN
        where many a sick person snowshoes it
across the ice to sweden with the cart... man!
snowman!, thirty below! me stove-hugging all day

(for Ylva Holländer)

petersburger hängun'

ins helle, ins allerhell
gehängt!, ein umfassend -jagd und aller
heilgen, november-aorta herbe angepackt (lies: a
lies ort, lies a), chaos im winterpalais, vor-
silbnwexl, -grad bleibt erhaltn, und neva strahlen-
schleier sowieso; ikone reingehackt: eines daniils
verlust: verlustig gegang eines charms (so ins
kyrillisch reingehackt ANGESCHWÄRZTE KO
PFBELAGERUN'/ein GPU-RANDHALTN, auch andre
ränder, andre existnzn(..); zuvor VON VELIMIR
NICHT DIE REDE zuvor bereiz schmerzlicher
eisnstein der unaufhaltsam die zarentreppe run
terrattert, sein unaufhörlich löwnwach zurückgespult glas
NOST IM ÜBRIGN HEISST »SCHNEIDETISCH«

(für Dieter Hiesserer)

jammed picture-wall, Petersburg

into the bright, into the allbright
hung!, a comprehensive -hunt and all
saints, November-aorta acerbly grabbed (read: an a
an ort, an a), chaos in the winter palace, fore-
syllable shift, -grad is preserved, and neva beam-
veil in any case; icon hacked in: loss
of a daniil: loss route of a kharms (so hacked into
the Cyrillic DEFAMATORY
HEAD-SIEGEan, EDGED OUT BY GPU, other edges
too, other existences (…); before VELIMIR GET
OUT OF HERE before already painful
Eisenstein who is unstoppably rattling down the
Tsar's steps, his unceasing lion-alertly spooled-back glass
NOST OTHERWISE MEANS "EDITING TABLE"

(for Dieter Hiesserer)

düsseldorfer kölemik

              sorgsam
gebräunt; blondiert im hautkot-
ürfummel, getrimmte zungen; flaumige
bällchen über den pfoten, die
kahlen hinterteile GROSSZÜGIGER
HERR SUCHT DAME ZWECKS TAGESFREI-
ZEIT das stolzierte, das getrippelte,
mostertfarbne pisse sondern die ab
in regenhaut verpackt: zurecht-
geschorne silberpudel;
                (in anwalz-,
in zahnarztpraxen hängt penck
an der wand, "beschissene düssel
dorfer schule");
          HOCHGLANS, ABZÜGE
AUF BARYTPAPIER
             im wortgestöber,
getrimmte zungen, die schneenasen;
unter gedimmter neoninstallation
die beine schmeißen EINE HEFTIGE
NERVENREVUE; stöbernde lawinen-
hunde bei pöseldorfer longdrinks;
an der theke katastrophenkünstler,
kralle im fischgrät (marcel duchamp
rotiert)
       »reden wir mal fraktur«,
»klar, typisch steinbock«;
              die groupies
nippen am tequila, sunreis im grafen-
berger wald: im wildpark das ewige
rehefüttern POUSSIERLICHE SONNTAGS-
FOTOGRAFIE; »Auf der Hardt« ein
kinderspielplatz hexenbrennplatz,
recht spät (1738):
          »der Theufell:
…so in Gestalt eines schwartzen

düsseldorf confidential

                         carefully
tanned; blonded in the haut cout-
ure schmutter, tuned tongues; downy
puffs over their paws, the bare
hindquarters GENEROUS
GENTLEMAN SEEKS LADY FOR DAYTIME
LEISURE the high-stepping, the dainty trips,
they secrete mustard-coloured pissings
packed in a waterproof: silver-
poodle with hair-do;
                         (in law,
in dentist practices penck hanging
on the wall, "shitty düssel
dorf school");
              HIGH GLOSS, PRINTS
ON BARYTA PAPER
                    in the flurry of words,
tuned tongues, noses full of snow;
under dimmed neon installation
banging one's knees A VIOLENT
NERVY REVUE; prying snow-
sleuths over long drinks à la pöseldorf;
at the bar catastrophe artists,
claw in herringbone (marcel duchamp
is swivelling)
               "let's get down to brass tacks",
"of course, typical capricorn";
                         the groupies
sipping at tequila, sunrise in the grafen-
berger wald: in the wildlife preserve forever
feeding the deer SPRIGHTLY SUNDAY-
PHOTOGRAPH; "Auf der Hardt" a
playground, witch-burning ground,
very late (1738):
               "the Dhevil:
…that in the shape of a black

Mans . . so eine raue Mütze undt . .
stumpfe schuen angehabt"; das lodert
vorm unabgeholzten forstrest, kopf-
rest gründlich ausgeschildert! KEIN
MOHN UND/ODER GEDÄCHTNIS!
ab jetzt
huschen meerkatzen durch deinen
kopfzoo, glotzen aus deinen grünen
augen, aus meim meerkatzenaug blick
ich dich an: wir alle werden grüne
augen haben (…);
                    schützengrün, schweiß;
torkelndes schützensilber, das peloton
legt rotgesichtig an; geflüsterte
bordelladressen, im wespenmonat
schießen sie den vogel ab
            HOCHGLANS,
LICHTEMPFINDL FILME, ABZÜGE AUF
BARYTPAPIER
            »wodka ist angesagt . .«

man... as had a shaggy cap and...
blunt shoes on"; crackling
before the relic of uncleared forest, her head-
rest covered in signage! NO
POPPY AND/OR MEMORY!
from now on
meercats dash through your head
zoo, goggle out of your green
eyes, I look at you
from my meerkat eye: we will all have
green eyes(...);
                    rifleman green, sweat;
staggering marksman-silver, the squad
aims with flushed faces; whispered
brothel addresses, they shoot
the trophy down in the wasp month
                             HIGH GLOSS,
LIGHT-SENSIT FILMS, PRINTS ON
BARYTA PAPER
                "it's time for a vodka..."

gestümperte synchronisation

in erster linie, in also vorderster
unter der stirnfront;
                        zunächst nur
stellen stellenweises auftreten zöge-
rndes hinzutreten der bilder, mehrere
anblicke nachundnach, eingeblen-
dete bananenschalen;
                        sichtlich gefälschter
flaggensatz: bei vortretenden augn (sichtbar!)
das katapultieren hereinkatapultieren
der blickkolportagen, unüberschaubare
wimmelbilder, bildgewimmer (reicht mein
pidgin aus?), undeutliches bis über
den hals bis längst übern kopf gepaddel
gefuchtel wüstes schlagen mit die arme!
das ist die sehnot, wies einen reinreißt,
exzessiv, wies ein runterreißt, gerade-
wegs sehnot, verheerend! AUF BEISPIELE,
KLAMMERN SIE SICH AN ANDERE MÜNDER UND
LIDDECKEL, AUF ANDERE BEISPIELE MUSS
HIER VERZICHTET WERDEN

slipshod dubbing

in the front row, so in the forefront
under the forehead;
                              at first just
spots sporadic arrival hesi-
tant adding of images, several
shots one after the other, cut
to a banana skin;
                              visibly false
flags run up: with eyes bulging out (visibly!)
the catapulting inwards catapulting
of the visual pulp, confused
teeming images, images teeming (is my
pidgin good enough?), up to your
neck in indistinct far over your head paddling
thrashing wildly beating your arms!
that is the urge to look, how it rips you in,
out of order, how it rips you under, out-
right urge to look, devastating! FOR EXAMPLES,
PLEASE LATCH ON TO OTHER MOUTHS AND
EYELIDS, AS OTHER EXAMPLES CANNOT
BE ADDED HERE

zivildienst. lazarettkopf

zur decke gerichtet;
aus urnenaugen (»alzheimer und
parkinson«) blicken die
bettlägerigen uns an, an uns
vorbeisterbend;
geflutete schützen
gräben, »monatelang rattenschlaf,
die bajonettangriffe..«; drahtverhaue,
spanische reiter; sich verarbeitende
krabbelnde tanks; in heizungskellern
angeschlossene verhörkabel; durch
brochene panzersperren, eingekoteter
luftschutzwart;
auf gezackten (zackigen)
photographien GEBLIEBENE UTENSILIEN
die ungesunde haut, übermüdete stimmen;
messer und anker zusammengesunken,
gestärkte schwesterntracht, daran
die rotkreuzbrosche ein verbandsplatz
(»kreuzburg/ oberschlesien«);
in den frisch-
bezogenen laken gebunkert die bomben-
nächte, nähte, UNBEWALTIGTES KOPF
LAZARETT, LAZARETT-KÖPFE daraus
die flammenwerfer speien, gespiene
kindsverluste der trümmerfrauen (»als
feuerwehrsmann vor -grad; unaufhörliches
flammenspiel, die frauentrümmer«);
in schleiflackregalen erblindete
kegelpreise, gedenkteller und
polierte -münzen; den feldstecher
vor augen, gekitteter reservistenkrug
oder gesplitterte fliegerbrille (»hab
mein leben nur wechselschicht
gekannt«);
auf der pflegestation
("zwoter schlaganfall und wund-

noncombatant service. infirmary head

               aimed at the ceiling;
out of urn eyes ("alzheimer's and
parkinson's") the bedridden gaze
past us, dying past us;
                    flooded
trenches, "for months no proper sleep,
the bayonet attacks..."; barbed-wire entanglements,
tank traps; tanks getting bogged down,
scrabbling to get forward; in furnace basements
wiretaps; penetrated
screens of armour, air raid warden
sealed in shit;
             on jagged (peaked)
photographs REMAINING BELONGINGS
the unhealthy skin, overtired voices;
daggers and anchors sagging inwards,
starched nurse's uniform, on it
the Red Cross pin a field dressing station
("kreuzburg/upper silesia");
                    bunkered
in the freshly-made sheets the bombing
nights, seams, UNPROCESSED HEAD
INFIRMARY, INFIRMARY-HEADS out of which
the flamethrowers spit, spat
lost children of the ruins women ("as
a fireman by -grad; the flame show
never stopping, the ruins of women");
on layered lacquer shelves blinded
skittles prizes, memorial plates and
polished medals; field-glasses
to the eyes, mended reservist's mug
or starred aviator goggles ("all I've
known all my life is moving
shifts");
           on the ward
("second stroke and bed-

gelegen, faustgroßer dekubitus")
die essensgerüche, scharfen
putzmittel und urin;
auf den (nacht)
tischen dünnen besucherblumen aus;
in zigarrenkisten gehortet: die
rostenden orden, eisernen kreuze
DAS GANZE WELTKRIEGS-TALMI,
VERSENKTER NIBELUNGENSCHATZ, DIE
LETZTLICH GEBLIEBENEN UTENSILIEN!
ach, faltige heimatschüsse, stümpfe,
entmündigte witwentrauer anekdoten
der toten

sores, a hole as big as your fist")
the food smells, acrid
cleaning fluids and urine;
on the (night)
tables visitors' flowers dry out;
hoarded in cigar boxes: the
rusting medals, iron crosses
THE WHOLE WORLD-WAR-TAWDRY,
SUNKEN NIBELUNG TREASURE, THE
FINALLY REMAINING BELONGINGS!
ach, wrinkled go-home wounds, stumps,
disallowed widow-grief anecdotes
of the dead

(»penzinger schreittanz«)

                              gaumen-
segel gehißt, schutzengelchen
abgedreht: den würgeengel installiert
bei ignorierter warnvorrichtung; häß
liche botschaftn langen ein ("hand-
habung wie immer");
                         überlagerte bänder!,
fading, stimmband gekappt, auch der
zum schweign gebrachtn landschaftn;
aus der membran, gekrächzter kehl-
kopf: die trauermessage, entstellter
hergekrächzter code (in fliegendem
wechsel auf den kaminsimsen der krähen-
vocoder); einstweilen unbeschadete
-nische hier, engerwerdende kluft ZU-
GESCHÜTTETE IM KOPF BIOTOPE:
                                knir-
schend unter den schuhen verschüttungen,
mexikanische brocken, weggesacktes kranken-
haus; am vierten tag dann kehliges röcheln die
hechelnden retter konnte man hörn, umsonst
anschlagende hunde und frierend die ratlose
hundertschaft überm rastlosen atem überm
rest DIE FREMDERWERDENDEN VERSCHLEPPTN
SPRACHEN, WACHSENDE SEUCHENGEFAHR, DIE
DÜNNERWERDENDEN STIMMEN: GEBEN
WIR ABC-ALARM

(für Reinhard Priessnitz)

("pavane in penzing")

                                      palate-
sail hoisted, guardian angels
turned away: the angel of wrath installed
ignoring the warning signal; ug
ly messages arrive ("same
processing as always");
                                      overlay of tapes!
fading, vocal chord severed, also of
the landscapes reduced to silence;
from the membrane, croaky phar-
ynx: the message of grief, displaced
croaked out code (in mid-air
relay on the chimney breasts of the crow-
vocoders); onetime intact
-niche here, a cleft getting tighter BIO-
TOPES BURIED IN THE HEAD:
                                  gna-
shing drift heaps under the shoes,
Mexican lumps, hospital sagging
away; on the fourth day then throaty rattling you could
hear the panting rescuers, dogs fruitlessly
rearing up and the muddled squadron
freezing over the restless breath over the
remains THE DEPORTED LANGUAGES
BECOMING MORE FOREIGN, GROWING DANGER OF EPIDEMICS,
THE VOICES GROWING THINNER: LET'S ISSUE
AN ABC-ALARM

(for Reinhard Priessnitz)

verkehrsfunk

anbei ein besonderer grün
donnerstag
       es nähert sich NOCH
NICHT IM BILD der ernste laichzug,
geduckte landfahrer; kriechspur
drauf zu, schon böschungsquerung
betritt unkend die bahn, schiebt
sich zur fahrbahnmitte JETZT IM BILD:
die komplette krötenwanderung! (geblähtes
spiegelglattes basedow)
           ach autobahn
kreuz, vergebliche manöver
               »heinz!
der wagen bricht!« (bei ins feld segelndem
vorderreifen); schons blech zusamm-
geschobn, verkeilt, entgrätete karossen;
-teile, gestierte rufe, rußhelfer
SCHÄRFER STELLN über teile stolpernde
seitenschneider, rettungssanitäter
GENAU IM BILD hinschlagend im löschschaum
im krötenbrei in gesperrter trümmer
landschaft (»viehische veranstaltung«)
»aufgespießt«, »glatt abrasiert«);
aus offnem wagenschlag dazu ein polkaschub,
verkehrsfunk meldet: »vorsicht
krötenwanderung«

traffic news

add on a particular
thursday in holy week
                              it's coming STILL
OFFSCREEN the serious spawn convoy,
low profile tramps; crawl trail
up to it, already crossing the embankment;
steps croaking onto the roadway, pushes
to the middle NOW ON SCREEN:
the full-blown toad migration! (swollen
mirror-smooth googly-eyed)
                              oh, the motorway
cross, useless manœuvres
                              "heinz!!
the car's coming off!" (the front tire skimming
into the field); soon the tincans crammed
up tight, wedged, filleted equipages;
-parts, bullish shouts, grimy helpers
SHARPER FOCUS stumbling over parts the
cutting crews, rescue medics
RIGHT IN THE PICTURE hacking in the extinguisher foam
in the soup of toads in the jammed ruin-
landscape ("a dog's dinner"
"impaled" "shorn clean off");
from an open door as well a burst of polka,
traffic news reports: "warning,
toad migration"

8. 3000er (Lawinenlicht)

diese wand:
lawinenlicht, harsche tiefkühlbox (»mittn
in der nordostwand«, »sauerstoffarmst«), die
zu durchsteign zu durch-
                    segeln, mitunter; wenn
wir uns di sturz, di absturzfotos anschaun
wolln (55?) des abgeschmierten kletterers, na
der im moränensalat, das eine weggeknickt das
grobe *sebastiangesicht* so überlaufm (»todesge-
tigert«, »endverdreckt« undsofort), gezackte
fifties halt;
            wir entsinnen uns
des heilgen bluter friedhofs, alpinistenlagerung,
fünfundsiebzik: di märklinplatte mit aufge-
klapptm glocknertod (»erfrorn aufgefunden«,
»in der pallavicini-rinne vom bl vom
blizz erschla«);
            ZIEMLICH MASSIV, lobn wir
das einlulln durch nebel, binnen weniger mi
nutn diese 200 m luft unterm hintern, gli
tschiggewordner griff im nu . . di
                    krematoriertn,
in urnen heimgekehrte söhne, gletschersalbe am
glas, lebenzrettende enziankküsse, runterge
stürzte obstlerflut UND DAS EDELWEISS UND
DAS EDELWEISS, beim klingeln in der
glübirne das alles das alles: IM
LAWINENLICHT

from: tiroltyrol, 23 part landscape photograph

8. 3000 metres (avalanche light)

                                  this wall:
avalanche light, encrusted freezer chest ("in the middle
of the north-east wall", "air thinnest"), to climb
through which to sail
                    past, occasionally; when
we want to look at the fall, the dive photos
(55?) of the pulped climber, ar,
the one in the moraine mess, the one snapped off the
coarse *sebastian face* so stained ("death-
stripes", "total writeoff" and so on), jagged
fifties actually;
              we recall
the cemetery of the holy blood, layers of climbers,
seventy-five: the model-railway layout with lid-open
glockner-death ("recovered frozen"
"in the pallavicini gully by the lie-
by the lightning str");
                FAIRLY MASSIVE, we praise
the dozing off in the mist, within a few mi-
nutes this 200 metres of air under your behind, sli
ppery hold in an instant ... the
                   cremated,
sons coming home in an urn, glacier
ointment on the glass, life-saving gentian kisses, knocking back
torrent of fruit schnapps AND EDELWEISS AND
EDELWEISS, at the tinkling in the
lightbulb all of that all of that: IN THE
AVALANCHE LIGHT

9. Gemäldegedicht Schruns

(» . . geb. 1894,
als Einj.Freiw.Untjgr. ALS
EINJÄHRIGFREIWILLIGER UNTER-
JÄGER am Pasubio für das Vater-
land gefallen 1916«);

grabfeldentsteigun', geflü-
gelte eskortn; dort drobn, klar,
wird jubiliert; ausweiskontrolle:
marterzeug;
       »gedt hin ier Vermaledeite«,
auf schub-, auf leichnkarren führt
beschwingt ein teufel das sitzende das
bremsnwollende, halbnackte menschliche
lamento dem feuer zu; von ungeheuern an-
gespien, di hände hoch!, beidhändig
spielkartn (3 herzn) wirft der hoch di
sich in seinen fingern krümmen, gleich
schon flammendes zurückgekohltes herz-
papier; wem, kopfüber in den pfuhl, vom
hochsprung niederkommend (fosbury-flop)
das leichn-, das lendntuch halb übern schen-
kel rutscht »Weh mier unzüchtiger Jüngling«
(SPRECHBLASN, FEUERBLASN IM SENSNGERECK »gehe
hin du unkeuscher (*unleserlich*)«; di opfer
an kettn von engeln gezerrt, oh grausam di
HIMMLISCHE BAHNPOLIZEI, hier noch mal strom-
stoß (lies: flammenschwert), »der kniet doch
noch drüber!«, geflügelt schlägt derda jetz
noch ma zu   jetzt schneit das jetzt matschig
jetzt kriechendes naß, das teilt sich: ein re-
chtes ein linkes, das obnunduntn, das teilt
sich di hiesige witterun'

(für Martin Gostner)

64

9. Painting Poem, Schruns

("…b. 1894,
as Einj.Freiw.Untjgr. AS
ONE-YEAR VOLUNTEER LIGHT INFANTRY-
MAN fallen 1916, on the Pasubio, for the
fatherland");

graveyard exit and ascent, wing-
ed escorts; for up there, up there, clearly,
is jubilation; i.d. check here:
martyring equipment;
                    "gang forth, ye Forspoken",
on push- on corpse-carts a devil
leads adagio the sitting the wouldbe
braking, half-naked human
lamento to the fire; spat on by
monsters, hands up!, two-handed
he throws up the playing-cards (three hearts)
crumpling in his grip, straight away
already flaming ash-withering heart-
paper; whose, head-first into the morass,
descending from the high jump (fosbury flop)
cere- or loincloth slips half
over their thighs "Woe to mee, a wayward Youth"
SPEECH BUBBLES, FIRE BUBBLES IN THE SCYTHE DODDERER
"forth thou unchaste (*effaced*)"; the victims
tugged on chains by angels, oh cruel-hearted the
HEAVENLY RAILWAY POLICE, here once again a voltage
surge (read: flaming sword), "he's kneeling
on it as well!", winged that one gets another
good shot in   now it's snowing now slushy
now creeping wet, that divides itself: a left
and a right hand, an upper and nether, it divides
itself, the local climate

(for Martin Gostner)

taunusprobe. lehrgang im hessischn

"Ich deutete abwärts: sie das rätselgesicht"
(Stefan George, 1922)

ssauntz   grölende theke.
ATEM-SCHUTZ-GERÄTE-TRÄGER-LEHRGANG was
für ssauntz! unter pokalen fuß-
balltrophäen die azurminiträgerin the-
-kn blond. –GERÄTETRÄGERLEHRGANG IN A.
springt kajal, dringt vor in kajal
kajalflor zu heavy metal sounz (vorher-
sage: grölender stammtisch), gerekktes
hinterzimmer-, jetzt gaststubn-"heil!!".
di theknmannschaft, pokalpokal, trägt
501 trägt wildleder-boots, drittklassiger
western den sie hier abfahrn HEILHEILHEIL!!!!
flaumblonde unterschenkel, es kajalt von
gegnüber; di blonde matte FUN!
                        AUGN – FUNK
IN B: FUNKSPRECHBERECHTIGUNXLEHRGANG, IN
C: FOLGT (*fig.* 3) DI MOTORKETTNSÄGE-
UNTERWEISUN', wies kajalt! hinpfeilnd aufs
dartboard, gewitterland-, gewitterlandschaft
im gesicht. die theknmannschaft (»1. preis
im torwandschießn 1990«) verchromtes hufeisen
im laredo-jeep, yosemety dschosmetti-aufkleb
an ihren niederkalifornien-karren, da draußn
vor der kneipentür. pfännchen-scheiß uber
hinkümmerndn topfpflanzen, hufeisnverchromt
man geht in bärenwiegeschritt (vorkraftkaum
laufn). der Große Feldberg, sendersender,
störfunk   ssaunnzz

Taunus sample. course in Hessian

"I pointed down: she the mystery face"
(Stefan George, 1922)

ssoundz.   bawling boozer.
DUST-FILTER-CARRIER-TRACTOR-COURSE what
soundz! under cups, foot-
ball trophies she wears an azure mini is
barmaid-blonde. – CARRIER-TRACTOR-COURSE IN A.
jumps uproar, thrusts forward in the uproar,
uproar plush for heavy metal ssoundz (fore-
cast: party bawling at the table), horizontal
backroom-, now saloon-"heil!!".
the boozer's own team, cupcup, wears
501s wears suede boots, third-rate
western they're putting on here, HEILHEILHEIL!!!!
fluff-blond back of thigh, the uproar from
opposite; the blonde hank. FUN!
                         EYE-RADIO
IN B: RADIO USER CERTIFICATE COURSE, IN
C, NEXT (*fig.* 3) THE CHAINSAW
LESSON, what an uproar! launching at the
dartboard, stormland-, stormlandscape
in their face. the boozer team ("1st prize
in parlour goal shootouts 1990") chromed horseshoe
in the Jeep Laredo, yosemity josemity-sticker
on their baja californiatrailer, stood outside
bar door. fryingpan-shit over
ailing pot plants, with horseshoes chromed
they roll in the Bear Walk (almosttoo
muscly to move). the Grosse Feldberg, trans-transmitters,
jamming signal   ssoundz

berserkr

di fingerspitze und di fliegen-
pilze; von letzteren JAJA ICH
ASSOZIIERE DAS von letzteren
di berüümtn-finnischn-wälder voll,
von suppentellergrööße, schreiendes
muskarin! von denen in mittlerweile
auch schon umgestülptn drööhnendn
wäldern konnt kaum mein augnfleisch
ich lassen: das nur aß mit, tja,
finnische fingerspizzn

(für die dichter nördlich von rovaniemi;
für alle tupilaks des hohn-nordenz)

berserkr

the fingertip and the fly-
mushrooms; of the latter YESYES I MAKE
THE CONNECTION of the latter,
the famed Finnish woods full,
big as soup plates, shouting
muscaria! from the in the meantime
already too turned inside out droooning
woods I could scarcely tear my eyes away:
did only eat that with, hmm,
Finnish fingertips

(for the poets north of rovaniemi;
for all tupilaks of the high north)

knirsch!

ratternde platte. wind-tape in
den kron. flekkiges *huschhusch* das
durch bänder zirpt: ein schädelge-
flakker, gestöber im anflug, stellen-
weise blindflug durchgeführt.
                              ARCHIVE
GEPLÜNDERT / GEPLÜNDERTE PLÜNNEN!, +
1 GAUCH NACH DEM ANDERN! split
tergrääm im unzerstörtn aug: balkn-ba-
lkn-balkm. im augn-, im -schauerraum
ein hin geplatschtes licht, schon
wieder zugeschattet: fott. ein zugeschü-
ttet, ausgeschlürft; ein-totes-paestum
das da rattert; -glifnplan, glifmplan o
or, organisazzjon TOTH, o GOtt

(für Oskar Pastior)

gnash!

rattling record. tape-wind into
the header. patchy *rushrush* that
chirps through the reels: a skull
flicker, flurry approaching to land, in parts
carried out by flying blind.
                    ARCHIVES
RANSACKED/ COSTUMIERS RENTSACKED!,
1 MUMMER AFTER THE OTHER! splinter
furrows in his good eye: beams-bea-
ms-beams. in the eye-, in the -auditorium
a splashed on light, already
shut by shadow again: gone. a banked-
in, sucked out; a dead paestum
what's rattling there; -glyph plane, chlieffen plan ee
ear, organisation TOTH, o GOth.

(for Oskar Pastior)

historienbild

landschaft mit flecken.
eine landschaft mit kirschflecken. eine
sich mehrende landschaft mit hügelketten.
eine in der ein alkoholiker-könig seinen
leibkoch an den bratspieß stecken läßt.
eine in der hussiten umkommen.
eine böhmische in der calixtiden (»?«)
und taboriten (»??«) sich abschlachtn.

landschaft mit kirschflecken.
eine in der hirsche bäume und wespen
umfallen. über die ketten unter knir-
schendem mond gehn. eine in der ein ober-
besazzer an stofffezzn in der milzz
schdirpt. flekkn. und, flekkn, eine über
die kettn unter knirschndm mont gehn. und
eine landschaft in der es wieder gehn wird.

history painting

landscape with patches.
a landscape with patches of cherry. a self
propagating landscape with ranges of hills.
one in which a royal alcoholic has his
personal chef stuck on the roasting-spit.
one where Hussites perish.
a Bohemian one in which Calixtids ("?")
and Taborites ("??") cut each other to bits.

landscape with patches of cherry.
one where stags trees and wasps
fall over. over which tank tracks go under a gna-
shing moon. one in which a reich
protector dies of tatters of fabric in his
spleen. patches. and, patches, one over
which tracks go under gnashing moon. and
a landscape in which it will prosper again.

von inneren minuslandschaften

gedächtnisprotokolle von gedächtnis. kuppen
temesvar ohren -15, zehen zehennägel -15, fuß-
sohlen augäpfel unbedeckt hermannstadt -15, tag-
der-autopsien -15 bedeckt, bauchräume kniescheibe
flatternd, dein hingestrecktes haar karpatenhaar.
besser kuckn minus wir uns das garnich erst
an. kamerafahrten in doppelbelegung, -belichtung brut-
kastenpferche. säuglinge notbeheizt, wirrnis und minus
im schwindenden blikk die letzte, gefuchtelte regie-
anweisun' c.'s (bedeckte sicherheitsangabe). zu-
ngnstrünke; -all-irm-inger. medienhimmel leuchtend
bei fünfzehn grad minus. da fällt c.'s pelzkragen-
coverleiche draus raus. gedächtnisprotokoll von
gedächtnisprotokollen von verflimmerten von
inneren minuslandschaften

of inner minus-landscapes

memorized notes from memory. fingertips
temesvar ears -15, toes toenails -15, soles
eyeballs uncovered hermannstadt -15, day-of-
autopsies -15 under cover, stomach area kneecap
flapping, your pushed-out hair carpathian hair.
better we don't even give the minus a look.
camera movements: in double -manning, -exposure stew-
ponds. sucklings emergency heated, confusion and minus
in our vanishing view the last, arm-swinging di-
rection from c. (safety reassurance from cover). to-
ngue stubs: ara hute ingers. media sky shining
at fifteen degrees below. then c.'s fur-collar
cover-picture corpse falls out of it. memorized notes from
memorized notes of glare-masked of
inner minus-landscapes

effi b.; deutschsprachiges polaroid

1

    endlostelefonate & lehm;
woran schei (»wo?, woran bitte?«)
                      di mo
mente di aufnahmen, di pralleren albn: o
vale photographien, apgefrühstükktn myrthn;
begrenzungn, uneingesehene zungn (»nie gelernt«),
gestopfter spül/beför-derunk na klar, im an
sazz verschwindet das, ist schon verschwundn he—
rztattoo urlaupsmunition AUSZEHRUN' wg. SCHRAN—
KW/ANT SCHLAFZIMMERHUND NEUM TEPPICHBODN (hier
fastzitat: »sehnsi di fototapete, breitwandschul-
dn sehn sie sich *das* an . .«); WORAN SCHEITERT MANDN

2

effi bekompt von ihrn mann   1 spülmaschine, elektr.
dosnöffner, bodystockings (= ›neumieder‹) und worte;
e. als (wider)wortmaschine, dida sagt sehnsuchtsehnsucht,
zu sich; effi macht sich zum abreißkalender, dabei
füllt sichs familienalbum, (…) JETZT,
BLAUSTICHIG, UNFOTOGRAFIERT;
                         »di mir gleich so
sonderbar aussahn weilsi strip pe hattn und drei- o
der 4mal umwikkelt u. dann eingeknotet und keine schlei
fe di sahn ja schon ganz gelb aus«

3

tablettnaugen, dazwischn grillabende o.ä. (zäheste dias),
das schnurrt so runter GEBUZTAGE, FILMRISSE, auch
etwas das sich häuft ER (zu nem freund): WORAN SCHEI-
TERT MAN DENN IM LEHM FRAGEZEICHN ÜBERHAUPT IMMER
NUR AN DER WÄRME

effi briest; german-language polaroid

1

       endless telephone calls and life;
at which appear ("where, where's it all, please?")
                                the in
stants the exposures, the more bulging albums: o
val photographs, breakfasted-on myrtles;
limitations, uncomplicit tongues ("never learnt that"),
clogged rinse/inlet   got it, in the
startup it disappears, has already disappeared heart
tattoo holiday ammunition PINING because of BUILT-
IN CUPBOARDS, BEDROOM DOG NEW CARPET (here
near-quotation: "look at the photo wallpaper, super screen
on instalments   look at *that*…"); WHERE'S IT ALL GONE WRONG THEN

2

effi gets from her husband 1 washing machine, electr.
tin-opener, bodystockings (='modern apron') and words;
e. as (contra)word machine, that says yearningyearning
to herself; effi turns herself into a tear-off calendar, and
fills up her family album (…) NOW,
BLUISH TINGE, UNPHOTOGRAPHED:
                              "which looked str
ange to me right away because they had wrapped
bandaid round three or four times & then tied in a knot and no
bow they were looking quite yellow already"

3

pill eyes, in between barbecues or similar (toughest transparencies),
it just chugs straight down BIRDAYS, FILM RIPS, also
something that piles up HE (to a friend): WHAT GOES
WRONG IN LIFE QUESTION MARK IT'S ALWAYS
THE WARMTH DOES IT

porträt JB. fuchspelz, humboldtstrom, tomatn

(ca. '72)
düsseldorf, aufm schadowplatz. eines
vormittags, im niesel. hinterm tapezier-
tisch im fuxxpelz im mantel. hab ich so
aus einiger entfernung hinter flugzetteln
gesehn; da macht ich BLAU eines vor-
mittags unter -strom

(ca. '75)
humboldtgymnasium, düsseldorf. ich sachs
euch: WIR BEKAMN HUMBOLDTSTROM. doktor
august peters, (GESCHICHTE) zu meinem zuspät-
kommendn freund roehle: ZIEHN SIE DEN BEUYS
AUS! SEIN MANTEL WAR GEMEINT.

('77)
kassel. installation der HONIGPUMPE. ein-
leitung von sauerstoff, daß honigfluß wir
sehn konnten. mittags, vorm friderizianum
bat ich den lagernden mann bat ich die angler-
weste um den tagschatten gibst du mir
die TOMATN und kam zu mir sein tomatnhant!

portrait JB. foxfur, humboldt current, tomatoes

(ca. '72)
düsseldorf, on the schadowplatz. one
morning, in the drizzle. behind the trestle
table in the foxfur in the coat. i saw you so
from a little way off behind pamphlets
there I was SKIVING off one mor-
ning under -current

(ca. '75)
humboldt high school, düsseldorf. I'm telling
you: WE GOT THE HUMBOLDT CURRENT. doctor
august peters, (HISTORY) to my late-
arriving friend roehle: TAKE THAT BEUYS
OFF! HIS COAT WAS MEANT.

('77)
kassel. installation of the HONEY PUMP. in-
jection of oxygen, that we could see
a honey river. midday, in front of the friderizianum
I asked the packing-up man asked the fishing-
jacket for the dayshade will you give me
the TOMATOES and reached out to me his tomatoey hand!

di zerstörtn. ein gesang

1
herzumlederun'. schwere.
geschüzze.
          böschungen im schweren in
gescheuchtm mohn; wir haben lawinen, la-
winenstunden und ja und -jahre gehabt. wir
pflanztn uns auf, wir aufpflanzer von ba-
jonettn. di blutablaufrinnen, die kanntn
wir.

2
WIR LAGEN IN GROBEN GEGENDN. WIR PFLANZTN
TOD. WIR PFLEGTN DEN GESANG / WIR AUF-
PFLANZER VON EWIGEM MOHN / DER SCHOSS
AUS UNSERN HÄUPTERN UNS IN DEN GESANG
DAS NANNTN WIR: *herzumlederun'*! + schrienz,

3
rattnschlaf. so war ich deutscher, serbe,
franzose; wir wir wir. WIR STEKKTN UNS auf
unsre bajonette, fühltn uns und sangen für
den böschunxmohn   »todesanxxt?,

4
ja.: 2 mal:
als in den 20ern ich in offne see hinauszutreibn
drohte; als das meer mich *fast* genommn hätte. +:
INFANTRIE-ANGRIFF / schlacht a. d. putna; ru-
ssischer gesang noch als ich nachts 88 war. ihr
gegnübergesang; nur der fluß trennte uns nach-
dem wir umgeladn wurdn in hermannstadt ('16).«

5
hart umledertn herznz. unsere schwere.
geschüzze   so bricht der tag an di rattnnacht.
nächte nächte rattnmächte im böschunx-, im
ratten-mohn. wir sind noch WIR WAREN UNTER DER

the destroyed. a song

1
heart for leather. heaviness.
cannon.
          slopes in the heavy in
alarmed poppy; we had avalanches, had av
alanche hours and yea and years. we fixed
ourselves, we fixers of bay-
onets. the blood drain grooves, we
knew those.

2
WE LAY IN BACKWARD REGIONS. WE FIXED
DEATH UP. WE NURTURED SONG/ WE FIXERS
OF ETERNAL POPPY./ WHICH SHOT
OUT OF OUR HEADS INTO OUR SONGS
W CALLED IT: *heart for leather!* + shouted it.

3
rat sleep. so I was German, Serb,
French; we we we. WE STUCK OURSELVES on
our bayonets, felt ourselves and sang for
the poppy on the revetment   "scared to death?

4
yes: twice:
when in the 20s I was dragged out to sea
nearly; when the sea *nearly* took me
INFANTRY ATTACK / battle on the putna; Russ-
ian song still when I was 88 at night. their
counter-song; only the river between us after
we were transferred in Hermannstadt ('16)."

5
with hearts leathered hard. our heaviness.
cannon so the day breaks on the rat night.
nights nights rat forces in the revetment-, in the
rat-poppy. we are still WE WERE UNDER THE

WEISZN (*jiddisch, di mond*) da waren wir,
DAS WARNEN WIR. UMSONST-GESANG

6

unterm rattnmond kurz schlafende schlaflose
mordexpertn; WIR SCHLIFFN di spatn an und
übtn an lebendign kazzn; wir rattn wurdn
trainiert wi rattn. WIR SCHWEISSTN uns schlag-
ringe; WIR SCHWEISSTN auf allen seitn GEHN SI
IN UNSER MUSEUM auf allen seitn den bauernkriixx-
morgenstern. da, grabnkampf, verhaue,

7

brach di tagsonne ab, nebel-, geschüzznebel-
betreut im böschunxmohn, kaum kriegen, 88, wir
unsre tablettnkrallen zum schmalgelbn todmund.

8

WIR SCHWOREN auf unsre schrapnelle, blikkn
aus schwer zerlebten trauma-höhlen auf unsre lebnzz-
geschichte.
kaliber.   }   korps-chor (»WIR HÖRTN
kaliber.   }   DI ENGLEIN
kaliber.   }   SINGEN«)
geschichte.   }

9

bestelle, jahre später, grünoxidierte äkker;
deine pflugschar, bauer, knarrt in hülsen, schä-
del, handgranatsplitter. das knarrt in deinen
schlaf, rattnschlaf, den unbesänftigtn. so
blüht dir der böschunxsmohn ins herz ins starr-
umlederte, wo keine schwestermutter dich anhört
und hört; *di weiße* scheint in gräbnmohn, ameisene
schwere, geschüzzdonner der deine träume ja jahr-
zehnte später pflügt und schwere,
schwere schwere (!!!) . .

WHITE (*yiddish, the moon*) there we were,
WE WARN OF THAT. SONG IN VAIN.

6

under the rat moon sleep short sleepless
murder experts; WE WHETTED the spades and
practised on living cats; we rats were
trained up like rats. WE WELDED ourselves knuckle-
dusters; WE WATERED with sweat on all sides VISIT
OUR MUSEUM on all sides the peasants' revolt nailed
clubs. there, trench war, entanglements,

7

the day's sun broke off, mist cannon smoke-
served in the revetment poppy,
we can hardly get, 88,
our pill claws to the narrow yellow death mouth.

8

WE SWORE on our shrapnels, looks
out of heavily lived-in trauma-caves on our life-
history.
caliber   }   corps-choir: ("WE HEARD THE
caliber   }   LITTLE ANGELS
caliber   }   SING")
history   }

9

worked, years later, oxide-green fields;
your ploughshare, farmer, creaks onto casings, sku-
lls, handgrenade splinters. it creaks into your
sleep, rat sleep, not quietened. so
the revetment poppy blooms for you for your heart
into the stiff sheath of leather,
where no sister mother listens to you or
hears; *the white* shines in trench poppies, ant
heaviness, cannon thunder which yea tens of years
later does plough your dreams and heaviness,
heaviness, heaviness (!!!)...

ornithologisches zimmer

ENTKEHLTE PAPIERE; tannen entkehlt.
da zik-zik-ziks: ihr reines schnikkern!,
zimmer mit kehle, veranda-kehlenraum!
frechrotes buschig, dat eichhörnchen am
turnen. gekehltes zimmer! flockn-flockn-
flokkn. zimmer mit meise, zimmer mit ko
hlmeise (2), zimmer mit landendm kleiber.
zimmer mit ring mit ringeltaube, mein un-
beringtes zimmer. zimmer mit brüstung,
brust rostrot: ihre kehle-kehle! nachz +
früh, na, N.A.C.H.T.I.G.A.L.L. zimmer mit
eingebauter nachtigall. scheu beide. 16
gramm gesang! scheues kehlchen. zutrau!,
zutrau! kommt ran und futter gesang, wies
falockt das futter; mit rosinen, leinsam
nie! zimmer mit kleiber, zimmer mit klei-
ber. ihr 16-gramm gesang! wie exklusiv:
R!O!T!K!E!H!L!C!H!E!N!! mein zimmer mit
rotkehlchen. königszimmer! du bist mein
kühlervogel (»ober. sekt jezz«) für mein
rotkehlchen + mich. für meine RR emilii bron-
tiih. beide : schön

ornithological room

GUTTERLESS PAPERS; cored pines.
there tsik-tsik-tsiks: their pure cluck!,
room with a throat, veranda-voice-box!
bold red bushy, the squirrel at airs
in twirls. grooved room! flakes-flakes
flakes. room with finch, room with tit-
mouse, room with great
titmouse (2), room with landing nuthatch.
room with ring with ringed dove, my un-
ringed room. room with breast-puffing,
breast rust red: its throat-throat! nights +
early, nigh, nightingale room
with built-in N.I.G.H.T.I.N.G.A.L.E. both shy. 16
grams of song! shy little throat. trust!,
trust! come close and feeding-song, how
the feed draws it; with raisins, linseed
never! room with nuthatch room with nut-
hatch, its 16-gram song! how exclusive:
R!E!D!B!R!E!A!S!T!! my room with
robin. kingly room! you are my
cooler bird ("garçon. champagne now") for my
robin + me. for my RR emilii bront-
iih. both: beautiful

blikk durch geöffnetes garagntor

nebeleisern blix: der jeepmann
garagn- und schußherr der da zu-
rrte, jagdgrün; in meim 11jährign
rükkn ein hochneblichter tannan-
stieg,   vor mir dies: HIRSCHGARAGE!
GARAGNWANT ALS HIRSCHWANT!, schon ap-
gesägtn geweihs der unbeschienene hu-
bertuskopf, des hirschkopfs augnfleisch
kopfunter, ausgependelt. da allgäuer
zerrnebel beidseitig raus, und aufgebro-
chn ausgeweidet ausgeräumter leib BO-
RSTIGE RAUMTEILUN' bei weggeräumtm
innereieneimer stark!!riechende -wände (g-
ruchsklaffung): der da   so hinge-
hängter hingeklaffter hirsch

look through opened garage door

foggy iron gleam: the jeepman
garage- and shoot-master who was strapp-
ing up there, hunting green; at my 11-year-old
back a deep misted pine
rise,   in front this; STAG GARAGE!
GARAGE WALL AS STAG WALL!, antlers al-
ready sawn off, the not shining Saint Hubert
head, the stag's head's eye meat head
down, dangling off. there Allgäu
curtain mist away on both sides, and breached
gutted voided body BRIS-
TLING SPACE DIVISION with cleared away
innards bucket strong!!smelling -walls (gap-
ing smell): the there   so, hung-up
gaping open stag

landschaftsdurchdringun'

aneignung ihres werkzeux; stoff-
betrachtung, betrachteter tra
chtnstoff (»etwa . . durchs föhn-
fenster lehnt sich der august«);
                                        weich
das haar in zungenrichtung: ich lecke di
achsel des sommers; der sommer ist eine frau

landscapepiercing

acquisition of their tools; inspecting
materials, inspected reg-
ional cloth ("pretty much ... August leaning out
through the mistral-window");
                                    the hair
soft in the direction of the tongue: I lick the
armpit of the summer; the summer is a woman

valkyriur. neuskaldisch

                              du-
rchtrennte luft, die waagerechte.
allmählich parabel-, dann kurvenbeschreibend
die zeugleiber. schön schneidende einstellerinnen
von schlüssen. über äugendn geysiren vor-
schießend ihre geysiraugn. ein dahinjagen! der
aufsitzendn, der insassen; in zerhufter luft
keuchende pferdeseelen: EIN BLUTBILD DIES, DER
STERBENDN ATEMWEG. (*schwerleserlich*) nordmeer,
schönheulend (*in etwa*), dahindüsende wälder, wald-
stükke weltstükke, schrammend, übersauster interalt.
für was für eine schlußeinstellung sorgen valkyriur!
(*nicht nur unleserlich: befallner passus*) valkyriur!
sturm, halsadern von bleistiftdikke, entfallende passage
geplatze nähte rauhnähte, die senkrechte sodann. flug-
zeugleiber im wie-ein-stein; im stürzn abstürzn noch
auf die auslöser drückend, grelle hälse, verwackelnd,
scheißend in vielsprachigem stoßgebet bevor im grunde
das alles hinterhältig endet. ohne einen gesang.

valkyriur. neo-skaldic

                               di-
vided air, the horizontal.
gradually describing parabolas, then curves
the craft bodies. beautifully cutting setters
of closures. over gaze of geysirs shooting
out their geysir eyes. a rushing! of
the riders, the occupants; in hoof-cut air
panting souls of horses; A BLOOD PICTURE THIS, PATH
OF THE DYING BREATHS. (*barely legible*) north sea,
beautiful howls (*in something like*) away-jetting woods, wood
parts world parts, scoring, hiss over ambush.
what kind of a terminal setting do valkyriur arrange!
(*not just unreadable: a lost passus*) valkyriur!
storm, neck veins thick as a pencil, diminuendo passage
burst stitches rough stitches, the vertical next. air
craft bodies in like-a-stone. in falling crashing still
jabbing at the buttons, shrill necks, unstable,
shitting in multilingual bursts of prayer before at the bottom
everything ends maliciously. without a song.

autopilot. phrygische arbeit

geregeltn flugs. vom kreiseln trudeln
abschmiern vorne keine rede. das also
bis-der-sprit-ausgeht; ohne lande-
erlaubnis di geschichte. ein irgendwie
alles, nix wissn groß. orient irgendwi,
stadtgründungen staatsgründungen wir
überfliegn das, hams schon überflogn.
cockpit völlig ohne orientierun', bei
zitterndn zunehmnd gezittertn armaturn-
nadeln; allerhand lämpchn; birnchnge-
flacker, ziemlich viel rot/grün.
       hinter
supercoolen pilotnbrilln di hightech-
richthofens am palavern, augapfelfarbe
pupillngröße unkenntlich. hintn wird
gezogn was-das-zeuch-hält, alles super-
besoffm, beschwichtigende stewardeß.
staubfarbenes untn, irgndwi orient. ein
flußlauf, vermutlich halys (verflogn?)
oder tigris-geschimmer. ein blutstrom
scheint auf (und verschwindet): ent-
seelte heere mit sich führend, leibert-
eile, glitschiges entgleitendes treibgut.
dann wieder wolknbänke, weiter nullsicht,
ekbatanas sonne schwarz unterm shador,
reichsheere rennend, fliehende gegendn,
vorn: sturheil der ihr schlachtnlenkerblikk,
sonore stimme die sich meldet; ein hier-
spricht-ihr-kapitän: ». . kapitän moira,
gläserne kanzel, wir überwindn gerade
gordion, ninive 40 grad celsius,
sonne strahl-strahl, null
warteschleife«
(verflogn).

autopilot. phrygian ware

steady course. no hints of
rolling, dragging, lubricating up front. this then
till-the-aviation-fuel-runs-out; no perm-
ission to land is the story. a somehow
everything, can't tell big. oriental somehow,
foundings of cities foundings of states we
fly over them, have already flown over.
cockpit wholly without navigation, with
twittering increasingly jittered indicator-
needles; lights on everywhere; bulb-
flicker, rather a lot of red/green.
                                   behind
supercool pilot shades the hightech-
richthofens in a palaver, eye colour
pupil size invisible. in the cabin
issuing anything that pours, all super-
drunk, soothing stewardess.
dust-coloured below, somehow oriental. a river
course, presumably the halys (flown by?)
or tigris-shimmer, a river of blood
shines up (and vanishes): carrying
lifeless armies with it, bodyp
arts, slippery streaming wrack.
then cloudbanks again, zero visibility,
the sun of ecbatana black under the chador,
imperial armies running, provinces in flight,
up front: stalwart the gaze of the governor of battles,
resonant voice announcing itself; a this
is your captain speaking: "…captain moira,
glass cockpit, we are now passing
gordium, 40 degrees celsius in niniveh,
sun beaming-beaming, no
landing stack"
(flown by).

schwarze sylphiden

der ihre sprache, eins-a
ware; verstehn (wollen); kom-
plett kannitverstan. links
gestrüpp, grauwert, savanne.
(»lassie dreizehn sein, di zwei
kolossale tittchn, eins-a wa
kolonialer nabel, lichtbildner,
der ausm schattn tritt«) der
auf di bäuche fällt. münzgrosse
zierde überm schurz, narbnanordnungen.
narbnordnung auch über der stirn.
verschlossene, unbepflanzt ihre lippm,
aus irgend vorkrieg/nachkrieg VORZEITN
im rückblick mitbringsel, im schädel-
spind im sucher. schwarze sylphiden (13).

black sylphs

her there's speech, A-one
ware; to (want to) understand; to-
tal no spika. left
undergrowth, grayscale, savanna.
("let them be thirteen, the two
colossal tits, one-A
colonial navel, a photographer,
coming out of the shadow") who
falls on their bellies. a coin-sized
ornament above the grass skirt, rows of scars.
row of scars above the brow too.
tight, bare their lips,
from some pre-war/post-war PREHISTORY
in hindsight a present from a trip, in the skull-
locker in the viewfinder. black sylphs (13).

karner

die eine hälfte ist ziemlich
vollständig erhaltn. listn. sinds
andreaskreuze?, chromosomen?
gekreuzte klingn: erregte männer
auf schnaps, alte schlachtplatte
zu verkündn. gezeigtes, vollständig
geöffnetes fleisch, auch unpaarhufer-
fleisch, sicher. eine meisterzei-
chnun': die ebene, die andre hälfte,
als ätzung, im säureschutzmantel
das tal. truhenfertig. truhenfertig
zerlegter -plan. strich für strich
eine ebene hinterlassner nachrichtn.
ohne letztn brief das nasse tal (au).
gehetzt. (»die pferdeschädel sollen
im gebüsch stunk ham; gesichtetes,
gesichteltes rippchen«), (*botnhaft g-
hetzt*: »besiegtnschädel andi grossmastn-
der-wälder geheftet«). hinge-, hinunter-,
versunkenes fl-, die gegnd ein fleisch-
versunkener hauff. als sackgasse dead
end zeigt sich dies (truhen fertig?)
zerlegte moor; palisadndunkel. im text
weiterwatn, zäh; zählebig. palisadn-
gebiß das wotanshorstis, worthorstis
zu schützn vermeint (»intifada im links-
rheinischn«, »achwo: rechz der weser«),
ingwäonische wellentheorie die sich umbra-
schwappend bildet, undaförmiges über-
schwappn. der himmel ein blaues stadion.
-russnfront, boh, sehs noch vor mir.
voll alles mitte pferdeschädel. kleingeld
im sumpf, quintilius, geld im herzkarner;
das ist es: im bodn
losn.

ossuary

the one half is more or less
completely undamaged. lists. are they
St Andrew's crosses? chromosomes?
crossed blades: excited men
on schnapps, an old battle plot
to spread around. on show, utterly
opened flesh, also non-equine
meat, certainly. a Master drawing:
the plain, the other half,
as an etching, in the acid-proof coating
the valley. freezer ready. ready for the chest
dissected plan. stroke for stroke.
a plain of left behind results.
without a farewell letter the wet valley (lush).
harassed. ("the horse skulls are supposed
to have stunk in the foliage; sifted,
filtered rib"), (*hasty like a*
messenger: "skulls of the vanquished fixed to the
yardarms of the woods"). hung, downwards,
sunken fl-, the area a spot
sunk in flesh. this (chests ready?) dissected
moor shows itself as the neck of a bag, dead
end; palisade dark. wade on
in the text, grimly; tough to kill. palisade-
teeth the wodenhurst, wordhoardis
hopes to protect ("intifada on the left
bank of the Rhine", "actually: right of the Weser"),
ingvaeonic wave theory which shapes up
umbra-splashing, unda-shaped over-
slap. the sky a blue stadium.
russian front, bah, I can see it now.
everything full of horse skulls. small change
in the swamp, quintilius, money in the heart's ossuary;
that's it: in the bottom
less.

-passbild. (polke, »*the copyist*« , 1982)

»*monk at work . ., vor ort . .*«, buch-
stabiert wer, vermutet notker den
drittn. es ist restlicht-, restlicht-
verstärkung, lesart, schwebe;
                              links vorm
rand: pol/*über* p *rasur oder schmutz—*
flekk/zweites l *auf rasur/ vorher* ei
ausgewischt;
                    (…) vielmehr ein bild
sich macht, davon, im bildstaub; wa-
tnd. ich meine diese art *bildzerstäubun'*,
das vernissage-gestotter jetzt ma bei-
seite. wolknformation so ebnhin mit schütt-
rem fernkreuz(chn) versehn. eine frage
der sehkraft, da der schreiber, bildzer-
schreiber sich di talschau versagt, oder
di hohen stämme vorm tristhang. schreib-
instrument pinsel kompassnadel: das weist
richtung stirn; der hintergrund traktiert,
gewalkte farbe (»sagtnsi: übertragungs-
konzentration?«). ich lerne das wort ein-
passbild. eben. e *aus* a *korrigiert/*
dessn erster strich *durch übergesetztn*
punkt/ *getilgt ist*

identity picture (sigmar polke, *"the copyist"*, 1982)

"monk at work…, on the spot", some-
one spells, presumes notker the
third. it is low light, low-light
intensification, variant reading, oscillation;

         on the left
by the edge: pol/ *over the* p *erasure* or *fleck*
of dirt/ second l *on erasure/ before that* ei
wiped out;
     (…) rather is making himself
a picture, of it, in the picture dust; wa-
ding. I mean this kind of *picture aerosol,*
now put away the vernissage chatter.
cloud formation so casually equipped with
wispy far cross(let). a question
of eyesight, as the copyist, picture un-
writer forbids himself the view downwards, or
the tall trees before the cloud bank. writing
instrument brush compass needle: that points
in the forehead direction; the background worked over,
trampled colour ("they said: transfer
concentration?"). I learn the word visual tolerance.
that's it. e *corrected from* a/
its first stroke *is erased by*
a point/ *above it.*

stimmschur

es ist natürlich alles völlig naß; glätte von
nässe, von den ganzn zeigereien. von der
rede von fernigem, sozusagn. eine stimm-
schur vorgestoßener süße, in der unsere na-
men ausgesprochn werdn. haarwust, brauen-
verwüstung. unter dem schattn, deinem schattn,
den ich mit meinem gesicht (name) unterscheide;
nasses haar von der hand, gerangel in den atem-
ordnungen.
                augn und augnhöhlen. zeige,
zeig mir, während di montagejungens draußn
ihre elementa-bleche zu installieren suchn.
geschepper, gezittertes zimmer; unsere stimmen,
körper dringn auf einander ein. lichte fleckn. blick-
lake.
        in nässe zungnredn, eindringlicher gesang. das
is doch nich zu laut oder? goldlack-der-frühe der
übers lager wandert, eine wüste der gaumen, ein getrenn
der grenzn von den körpern der stimmen. dazu einiges
ausm ghettoblaster, sprecherin und gesang, das wechselt
im nassn sich ab.
                     stimmschur, süße!
der frühling: kadaver, lacktabelle im licht. deine haare, stern,
(beatmung), sind wi eine herde ziegn (zeigeherd), di auf dem
berge glatt geschoren!, das muß man sich, gezeigt, vor augn
halten und erlaubn. lacktabelle, timetable-der-körper! natürlich,
eine rose ist natürlich: rosen.
                helles schattnzeug
der stimmen, es regnet jetzt, getriefe, goldlack (wi gesacht) der
frühe, so redn wir. das licht jetzt, deiner augn,
wie ein ritz im granatapfel

voice fleece

of course everything's wet through; slick
with wetness, from all the showings. from the
talk about farness, so to speak. a voice
fleece of advanced sweetness, in which our na-
mes are uttered. turmoil hair, ravaging
of brows. under the shadow, your shadow,
which I distinguish with my face (name);
wet hair off the hand, wrangling in the ordinances
of breath.
                    eyes and eye sockets. show,
show me, while the fitter lads outside
try to install their all-weather roof.
clatter, trembling room; our voices,
bodies thrust against each other. patches of light. gaze-
sheet.
          in wetness talking in tongues, assertive song. that
's not too loud, is it? morning's gold lacquer which
wanders over the encampment, a waste of palates, a shed
of the borders of the bodies of the voices. along with something
from the ghetto-blaster, female voice and song, alternating
in the wet.
                    voice fleece, my sweetness!
the spring: cadaver, lacquer tablet in the light. your hair, my star,
(inhale), is like a herd of goats (show herd), shorn smooth
on the mountain!, one has to, shown, keep it in front of one's
eyes and allow it. lacquer tablet, timetable of bodies! of course,
a rose is natural: roses.
                    bright shadow-stuff
of voices, now it's raining, dripping, gold lacquer (as we said) of the
morning, so we say. the light now, of your eyes,
like a split in the pomegranate.

chaldäischer katalog

nachtwacht, kometin!, alter schnee!
zur nachtmitte, sommers, gezische.
lichtspeichelfährten, bollen eines
blauaufscheinendn bollids! wi-am-
schnürchn vorüberknickernde leucht-
spuren: seltener anblick, so eine
milchstraße, screen ächter tiefnwir-
kung. hinpfeilen; ein vorüberhechtn,
und, weites zurücklassn, streifiges
stehnbleibn, um zu verschwindn. wie-
der einer oder eine. schon verschwun-
dn. grad so hirschnsprung von hier,
gepfeif, »wie von nüstern«. also, daß
son pünktchn, geschwänztes, rüber-
pfauchndes pünktchn, der eine weile
(zeitnüster) stehenbleibt; und wieder
einer. kleiner. total besser als . .,
sagtn di altn nich: kolossal? der hoch-
getürmte *weiße striem*. ein fädnziehen.
durchzischter schnee. ohrlose wir,
weißäugig unter der decke.

chaldaean catalogue

night watch, cometess!, old snow!
in the middle of the night, in summer, hissing.
light spittle trails, volley of a
blue-gleaming bolide! as if marbles
flying by wire light tracers; a rare sight, such a
galactic screen of non-virtual depth-
effect. darting forward; bounding past,
and, far leaving behind, stripy
standing still, to disappear. another
one, he or she. already va-
nished. just like that a stag's bound from here,
whistling, "as if from horse nostrils". so, that
this sort of dot, tailed, hissing-
by dot, which for a while
(time's nostril) stops still; and another
one. a small one. totally better than…,
didn't the oldies say, cosmic? the tower-
ing *white slashes*. a pulling of strings.
hiss-pierced snow. us earless,
white-eyed under the blanket.

dermagraphik (kanaanäisch)

gazellen. gazellen-
haut, wi abgegriffn. darauf
schriftbilder, und auf ziegnhaut
und auf häutn von schafn; von
nagelgröße zehntausnd übrig-
gebliebene stückchn. wi si drüber
knien! etwa blindflug in den palimpsest-
wust. tierhautinschriftn, behaucht. welche
flüssigkeit. »südfrucht«, gehauche,
»südfrüchte!«, ins auge springnde,
beidseitig, stellen. ATEMANSTALT
(erschlossn). da

hat es uns nach uns verlangt.

dermagraphic (canaanite)

gazelles. gazelle-
skin, as if well-worn. on it
page layouts, and on goat vellum
and on sheepskin; of thumbnail format
ten thousand preserved pieces. how they kneel
over it! like flying blind into the palimpsest
tangle. creature fell inscriptions, breath fogged. what
a fluid. "southern fruit", breathing,
"southern fruits!", eye-catching,
recto verso, passages. BREATH INSTITUTE
(recovered). there

we felt a craving of us for us.

kopf, kragn

aufscheinender reif; irgendwo da, draußn.
innerlich verlaufsform, verlaufsformen, ver-
formungn von verläufn, weitschweifigster
nein: ungeschweifter haß, dies laufnlassn.
badeinlassn nebnan.
            reifnschein also. über
teurer auslegware kamera, handkameraeinsatz so
scheints über di hotelbildillustration, nur
ein so drüberhin: lichtgewechselte wand. kein
clip im dornbusch, wenn ich das richtich seh, **hu**-
mpelndn aux. soll ich? so. nein kein mein-
nessushemd-kratzt, kunzfaser. nichts was nicht
im interconti abginge (scheine).
              plötzlicher
rein, an di zwo schirmchn, platzender aufschein
einer tatsächlich brennendn, sehr bald schon
ins knie gehendn, tonlosn, gestalt; menschn
drumrum, eher kommentarlos; tosend, wies
scheint. raustosend aus den armaturen, hin-
äugndn munds; wasser, wassersturz, satter, ein
heißer atem darin, mitausgetriebene frequenz,
dies präparieren eines bads-am-samstagabnd.
federnd behüpfte auslegware, einbein-gehüpf,
di hose unterhose loszuwern; son hosenbild, **ho**-
telhosnbild, zischelndes drahtiges haar, und
klamottnsalat. züngelndes, jetzt, menschnbein,
verbissenes hüpfhüpf ebn, einziger brandfleck
der riesnmonitor, klapperndes schirmchn; in
hellen batzn wächst das grausn, in hellen **ba**-
tzn auf diesn körper hinschmelzndes, in ihn
hineinsinkendes, in den leib eintretendes, ihn
zu durchsintern scheinendes, bei fuchtelndn **fu**-
nkelndn gliedmaaßn: reifngummi und flammngemisch.

da füllt in hörbar plaudernd-satterem
tone di wanne sich, ganz ohne löwnfüße;

necklacing

suddenly shining tire; somewhere, out there.
in interior curve of process, curves of process, de-
formings of processes, most sweeping
no: indelicate hatred, this letting it run.
bath running next door.
                    tire shine then. on
dear display goods, camera, a hand-held passage it
would seem over the hotel glossy, just a
quick scan: light-shifted wall. it's not
an advertising clip in the veld, if I am seeing straight, **jog**-
ged too. should I? like this. no not a my-
nessus-shirt is itching, synthetics. nothing which
would not look right in the interconti (or seem to).
                               sudden

come in, on the two screens, bursting flash-up
of an actually burning, very soon to fall
on its knees, soundless, figure; people
round about, lack of commentary; raving, as it
seems. raving right out of his fixtures, his mouth
out on a stalk; water, rushing water, full, a
hot breath in it, a frequency sent out along with it,
this preparing a bath on saturday night.
buoyantly hopping display goods, on one leg,
to get out of the trousers and pants; such a trouser picture, **ho**-
tel trouser picture, hissing wiry hair, and
clothes made hay. convulsing, now, human leg,
obstinate hophop in fact, the giant monitor
one big scorchmark, little screen rattling; by
big clods the grue grows, in bright **clu**-
mps melting onto this body, sinking into
it, entering the body's door, seeming
to spatter through it, with thrashing spar-
king limbs: tyre rubber and flame mixture.

there the bathtub is filling in audible chattering-repleter
tone, quite without lion's feet;

ladn in allen intercontis in allen inter-
contis di löwm di löwinn zum bade zum **ba-**
de: der löw steigt gleich ein.
                                der kragn der
kragn. und, zum glück, tonlos, geruchlos
das restflammn; unter der napalmsalbe durch-
schwärztes harzherz, betanzt. restaufschein
der reif.
di augn wären schmelztiegel, wären
di -öfn? wären former durchformer des scheins,
widerschein des scheins? fangschlag den
bildern? gesang der jünglinge? chaldäischer
gestirne betrachtun'? totnfurz fürze ins
feuer? das schreim, zuletzt, verbenloser
rauch? da di tatze, wis scheint, jetzt
den knopf findet? drückt?

invite in every interconti in every inter-
conti the lions the lionesses to the bath to the **ba-**
th: the lion is just getting in.
                                   the collar the
collar; and fortunately, soundless, odourless
the dying flame; under the napalm salve black-
ened resin heart, danced around. dying up-flash
the tire.
the eyes would be crucibles, would
be the furnaces? be formers transformers of seeming,
catoptric of optic trick? a coup de grâce to the
pictures? a gesang der jünglinge? contemplation
of chaldaean stars? death-fart farts in
the fire? and writing, in the end, verbless
smoke? as the paw, it seems, is now
finding the knob? pressing?

serner karlsbad

wo in angesagter umgebun'
di zensur ihr sprudeln begann.

zentralgranitmassn.
geselchter schnee. nichts

wußte ich, zweiundsiebzig,
von einem haus edelweiß wo

mattkaiserschrunde oder ocker-
gestimmte, oder sonstwi-erinnerun':

»sprich deutlicher«
in karlovy vary

. . di (mittags?)sonne, geschwächt,
in spiegeln mitgeteilt wurd; wo

der becherovka in geschliffenen
gläsern und rede auf di marmor-

helligkeit knallte. karlsbad-sounds:
»o sprich deutlicher« in geselchtm

schnee, und »jedes hauptwort ein
rundreisebillet«.   SERNER

der ging von prag aus
gemeinsam ins gas.

serner, carlsbad

where in announced surroundings
the censorship began its babbling.

central granite massifs.
salted snow. I didn't

know anything, seventy-two,
about a House Edelweiss where

mattkaiser chasm or ochre-
toned or other sort of memoirs:

"speak up"
in karlovy vary

… the (midday?) sun, weakened,
was announced in mirrors; where

the becherovka rang in cut-glass
beakers and speech on the marble

gleam. carlsbad-sounds:
"oh speak up" in pickled

snow, and "every substantive a
return ticket"   SERNER

who went on the trip from prague
group ticket to the gas.

falknerei

»ich zôch mir einen falken«
Der von Kürenberg (1150)

eine geöffnete faust der himmel,
lederner dezember. in den
der greif (turmfalke, mauerfalke,
wespnbussard?) steigt und an
den sprachn rüttelt. rüttelnd
steht; di turmwand markiert
mit falknmist. ein weiß, wo,
weite, der abendstern
sich zeigt.

(für Albrecht Mauritius Wenner)

falconry

"I reared me a falcon"
Der von Kürenberg (1150)

the sky an opened fist,
leathery december. into which
the griffin (kestrel, tower falcon,
kite?) towers and shakes
at the languages. stands
shaking; the tower wall marked
with falcon droppings. a white, where,
wideness, the evening star
is revealed.

(for Albrecht Mauritius Wenner)

quellenkunde

1

genommene einsicht; kaum zu durch
schaun. eingedunkelte plattn di
sich übernanderschiebm, in leism
knirschn sich vernehmen lassn,
dennoch. ein langwieriger öffnungs-
prozeß: ei, eisnschlüssel (kinderarm);
eine waffe.
        und sind, notdurft augn-
gewöhnun', verhältnisse so sicht-
verhältnisse; quelle als schattn-
dasein. schlitzfenster nur, grünspalt,
alles zugerankt. und nahezu vernichtet:
glasplattn in schattnfeuchter schmiere.
verstümmelte (schimmel) daguerreotypie
einer ärztekammer, eines, wi-sagt-man:
ehem. Quellheiligtums.
geschundenes loch (geschindelte kapelle).

2

DI QUELLE. aber längst schon, damian,
verschwundn. DI QUELLE. das nichtmehr-
gefüllte, kosmas. DI QUELLE. hüfthohe
einfassun'; massiges steinbassin. da
ist nichts mehr zu wollen. einzige
feuchtigkeit der bau. gebröckel. grus.
ein abriß-piece. zu feucht, kein brenn-
holz, di klammgequollenen bänke; händ-
chn, beinchn, gebärmuttervotiv: nässe.
billige öldrucke, schiefe reste. das
bessere abgeräumt. das beckn. di leere.
di wasser. nässe. di reste.

spring lore

1
insight weakened; hard to see
through. darkened slabs riding
up over each other, making themselves
heard in quiet gnashing,
all the same. a long drawn-out opening
process: egg, iron key (barrenness);
a weapon.
        and relationships, remedial eye
-adapting, are visual
relationships; source as a shadowy
thing. just a slit window, green crack,
all overgrown. and almost annihilated:
glass panes in shadow-damp smear.
mutilated (mould) daguerreotype
of a consulting-room, a, how do you say,
former holy well.
shattered hole (shingled chapel).

2
THE SPRING. but long since, damian,
vanished. THE SPRING. the no-longer
filling one, cosmas. THE SPRING. coping
at hip height; massive stone basin. there
is no more you could want. the hut no more than
moisture. crumbling. pulp.
fit for tearing down. too damp, not fire-
wood, the benches swollen with dank; votive hands,
legs, wombs tiny: wetness.
cheap oleographs, tilted remnants. the
better stuff taken away. the basin. the emptiness.
the waters. wetness. the remnants.

nordkaukasische konsonantn

felsn stündn im kaukasus? im
kaukasus stehn hohe felsn.
                              vor
kurzm nie den namen noch gehört, so
brecher, zungn-, zeugnbrecher. brech
mir die zunge ab noch, zischn, sag ich,
sacht di gattin.
                    transporte, gar nicht
deklarierte holztransporte: sargholz;
holz, das schläft. oder gleich räum-
panzerstimmen, kettngesang, der di
zerteiltn zusammenschiebt; erdmassen
drauf. eisern. es stiemt.
                           sechs trinken
kühlwasser; atemlos der funk, atemlose
empfänger. ICH KANNS NICHT AUSSPRECHN /
totngestiem. und wespen. wespn!
di von lebern fressn.

north caucasian consonants

said cliffs rise in the caucasus? in the
caucasus rise high cliffs.
                              who
not long ago had never heard their names,
sort of twisters, tongue-, thingtwisters. I'm
still breaking my tongue off, hissing, I say,
says my wife.
                    shipments, quite unlicensed
timber shipments: coffin wood;
sleeping wood. or could be voices of
armoured bulldozers, tracks song, shoving
the dismembered together; masses of earth
on top. iron. drifts of snow.
                              six are drinking
water out of the radiator; the radio breathless, breathless
receivers. I CAN'T SAY IT /
vapours of death. and wasps. wasps!
who eat livers.

mithraeum

es ist der SOUND; entfernte hintergrund-
musik, dünnfließnd rausch; berieselung
zunächst, die sich mit knirschn (schrittn)
mischt, das fahle grün, der schwamm; zu-
unterst rausch SCHEINTOTER TRAKTE.
das frösteln, tintige mässiger helle, das
ausgependelt von der decke fällt. ein was-
sermürber putz, zerbröckelt BILDER-
LÖSCHUNG / RAUSCH. die träger. ho-
rizontalen säulenstümpfe. der vollgesogne
stahlbeton. weniger fern, von raum zu
raum, ist SOUND IST RAUSCH. der an-
schwillt, braust. und weiter flechtnkupfer,
grünstich klammer wände. wächst an und
draufsicht: verlautbarung von *echter quelle!*,
die, RHYTHMUS, hellgläserner schenkel
HALL hin zur kloake sich verschwendet.

mithraeum

it's the SOUND; distant background-
music, thinstreak rushing; trickling
at first, which mixes with crunching (steps).
the pale green, the mould; under
all rushing of DEAD SEEMING EXTENTS.
the shivering, inklike of moderate brightness, which
droops and falls from the ceiling. a plaster
softened by water, crumbling WIPE
PICTURE / RUSH. the supports. ho-
rizontal pillar stumps. the drenched
armatured concrete. less far, from room
to room, is THE SOUND IS RUSH. which
swells, showers, and further lichen copper,
verdigris of clammy walls. grows and
seen from above: the declaring of a *genuine spring!*,
which, RHYTHM, bright glassy joint
ECHO goes to the cloaca to disappear.

ruma. etruskisches alphabet

malariasümpfe, dampfnd vor bildern.
von anfällen, ausfälln hergenommen.
BILDERSÜMPFE aus denen namen
steign, geblubber, den figuren bei-
geschriebenes, wie:

fleischkeil, nebelbank über den
colli emiliani; hastunichtgesehn wird
rom di zunge abgenommen; rom wird
gestreckt, geteilt (liniert) und aufgekocht.
dies abgekochte rom; dem geben wir, zart,
seine zunge zurück. di wächst rom zwischn
den zähnen heraus: ein römisches züngel-
chn; romgezüngel! I MODI DI DIRE
ROMANESCHI UND DIE LECKT
länder weg; berginnen; sabinerberginnen,
etrurische geschmacksknospn; dazu das
getreide, di pferde etruriens, alles
gekauft.

ruma. etruscan alphabet

malaria swamps, steaming with pictures.
weakened by attacks, flakings.
PICTURE SWAMPS out of which names
climb, bubbling, captio-
ned to the figures, like:

flesh wedge, cloud bank over the
colli emiliani; didn't you see rome's
tongue is being taken away; rome is
stretched, divided (lined up), and reheated.
this sterilised rome; to which we, tenderly,
give its tongue back. that grows out through
the teeth of rome: a roman pointer;
rome tonguing! I MODI DI DIRE
ROMANESCHI AND THAT LICKS
countries away; mountain interior; sabine
mountain interior; etrurian tastebuds; then
the wheat, the horses of Etruria, all
bought.

Die Modefarben 1914

die modefarben von 1914 waren
Blumenfeld (Berlin/New York) zufolge,
waren diesem sprachen-fotograf zufolge
ziemlich zuerst:

nil.
ein grün natürlich, anorientalisiertes abend-
land, das großbürgertum hinter schweren
portièren. bei indirekter beleuchtung trägt
Berlin auf, was Paris trägt.

tango.
das orange. die trauer
früchte die den blick verkanten.

südfrüchte wurden kaum gekannt
sie kamen im beamtentume vor:
auf dem weihnachtsteller. auf dem
börsenparkett tango, schiffbau
stahl bestens notiert. und:

ciel.
ist der verdrehte himmel.
blue pills und stahlparkett.
zur frühjahrssaison natürlich

von marne gar noch nicht
die rede. ab herbst war dann
das kleine schwarz natürlich
angesagt.

kleines schwarz.
schwarztöne, di allgemeiner wurden;
besagte zunahmen, zunahmen, in dem maße wie die herzgruben und
-töne schwacher, dann weg- und abgeschaltet wurden. und
die listen ("ciel") sprachüberlagert von namen und

The Colours in Vogue, 1914

the colours in vogue in 1914 were
according to Blumenfeld (Berlin/ New York),
according to this speech-photographer
more or less first:

eau de nil.
a green naturally, oriental-tinged West,
the grande bourgeoisie behind heavy
shutters. in indirect light Berlin
presents what Paris is wearing.

tango.
orange. the fruits
of mourning which soften edges of the gaze.

southern fruits are hardly known
they were bought by officials:
on the Christmas plate. on the
stock exchange floor tango, shipbuilding
steel at bullish prices. and:

sky blue.
is the sky turned inside out.
blue pills and steel flooring.
for the spring season of course

no mention yet
of the marne. from autumn on
the little black number was of course
a big seller.

little black number.
shades of black, which became more widespread;
they increased, increased at the rate that the heart-pits and
-sounds grew weaker, then were turned down and off. and
the lists ("sky blue") speech-overlaid with names

abersprachn. noch war die grippe
nicht in sicht

laufsteg laufgraben.

den toten wie den witwen, immer in den nachrichten,
immer voll drauf, voll zwischen die beine gefilmt und –

noch waren skagerrak und grippe
nicht in sicht. die tödlichen kawenz-
männer im seitengespiegelten ciel:
»feuer!«, »kaltes wasser!«, »gas!«

ab sommer-, apper herbstsaison:
schwarzer wollcrêpe (gekappt)
schwarzer baumwollcrêpe, kappen,
schwarzer taft.
baumwolltüll, velourschiffon
alles schwarz. herbstbläue über den städten und schlachtfeldern,
schwarzer baumwolltüll.
schwarzer velourschiffon, darf ich mal,
für das tiefdecolletierte schwarze abendkleid
das mit der schwarzen spitzn-
(gekappt)

gesprächsunterbrechung durch
unrhythmischn *historiker*. zerstreut
wirkt dies durchgesuppte sprecherchen und
bammelmann, fidel wie die erhängtenleiche,
mit seinem:

»nix nil, nix tango. ohne ciel oder unter freiem
himmel. oder-oder, oder nich mehr so jetzt. spr-
rache über projektile, blue pills, blaue bohnen wohin
man tritt, das is sprache! oder
was andres.«

and counter-languages. the influenza was
not yet in sight

catwalk communication trench.

for the dead and the widows, always in the news,
always directly on, filmed fully between the legs and –

Jutland and influenza were
not yet in sight. the deadly freak waves
throwing sky blue side-reflections:
"fire!", "cold water!", "gas!"

from summer, from the autumn season on:
black wool crepe (edit)
black cotton crepe, edit,
black taffeta.
cotton tulle, velours chiffon
everything in black. autumn blue light over the towns and battlefields,
black cotton tulle.
black velours chiffon, may I,
for the deep-décolleté black evening dress
which with the black lace-
(edited)

conversation interrupted
by unrhythmic *historian*: this
soaked through speakerette and dangling man
seems distracted, loyal as the hanging cadaver,
with his:

"none of the eau de nil, no tango, no sky blue or under open
skies. either-or. or not quite that now. sp-
eech over projectiles, blue pills, blue rounds wherever
you tread, that is speech! or
something else."

wo. im.
wo im anderswo die
herztöne kenntlich wern. blin-
kende kennung. kennungen der landschaft.
der landschaftn, die flußnamen abhorchen.
sumpfgebiete. gebirge. oder andere
AUFFALTUNGEN VON FLEISCH: VON FLEISCH
EIN VERPLOMBTES JAHRHUNDERT

weitere und weitere auffaltungen:
die aufdrucke (parole) auf den eisernen rationen;

die aufwerfungen von erde, etwa die querung
steiniger bachbetten. gebüsche. buchen, birken,

tannenwälder. beschuß an reißenden flüßn. im
lehmbett, in nässe: wie die gestammelte briefschaft
durchweicht. diese zeilen, dieses ziehen in der
schulter: dieses werfen. diese abzieh-gräbn, soweit

reichen die – wieweit reichen die ohren? wieweit
reichen meine ohren: meine augn festgefressn.

die augen im weichen blei watend staubiger briefe.
ein waten in tintenstift. aussagefähige stegographie.

zuhackende amtsschreibmaschine. perforierungen,
hier und da der papierkörper. sichtbar der sonnen-

schein, der die quellen alle überstrahlt. im graphit.
form: die karpaten als schnee-emblem, gebirgs-

emblem. schmauchspuren über gesicht und stadt.
der großvater (32) kommt. ruhrkrank kommt er

vom isonzo-lazarett zurück – weihnachten 1918.
steif von blut und siff die kaiserliche uniform.

die augen, die gesichtswerkzeuge, kauwerkzeug
in tätigkeit. die entsetzte mutter hört: »wenn

where. in the.
where in the elsewhere the
heart shades become recognisable. flash-
ing callsign. callsigns of the landscape.
of the landscapes, intercept the river names.
swamp regions. mountains. or other
RUCKED-UP CREASES OF FLESH: A STOPPED
CENTURY OF FLESH

wider and wider creases:
the stencils (slogan) on the iron rations;

the thrown-up heaps of earth, maybe the crossing
of stony stream beds. bushes. beeches, birches,

pine woods. bombardment on rapid rivers. in the
clay bed, in wetness: like the stammering letter
sodden. these lines, this tug in the
shoulder: this throwing. these drainage-trenches, they

reach so far – how far do the ears reach? as far as
my ears reach: my eyes bitten fast.

the eyes wading in the soft lead of dusty letters.
a wading in indelible pencil. meaningful encryption.

pecking office typewriter. perforations,
here and there in the paper sheets. visible the sun-

shine, which beams on all the sources. in the graphite.
form: the Carpathians as snow-emblem, mountain

emblem. smoke traces on face and town.
my grandfather (32) comes. with loose guts he comes

back from the isonzo-field hospital – christmas 1918.
the imperial uniform stiff with blood and dirt.

the eyes, the sight equipment, chewing equipment
in action. the indignant mother hears: "if

uns hoffmann keine anderen gibt.« also: mal alle

herhörn! »ihre herztöne und alles, ihre sprachn
alles haben die sich, sich selber weggehorcht.«
rhythmische *historia*.
nicht weniger absent ist diese *sprecherin*:
das war, mit photos von Blumenfeld,
der farbenanfall für 1914; entschuldigen
möchten wir uns für den

totalbildausfall

hoffmann won't give us any others." so: everybody

listen to me! "their heart shades and everything, their languages,
they have listened everything, away, from themselves."
rhythmic *historia.*
this *female voice* is no less absent:
this was, with photos from Blumenfeld,
the colour range for 1914; we would like
to apologise for the total

loss of picture

Bienen, eine Wespe

nec miseros fallunt aconita legentes
auch werden von eisenhut die armen sammler
nicht gefoppt
Vergil, *Georgica*, Buch II

mit haaransatz ein bergwald, der sich hören läßt. pilzsammler, sucher
im staub der forststraße, der runtertrampen will ins tal; nichts hatter

gefunden: »trocken wie die wüste gobi!«, im wagen verbindet er sich
die hand mit dem taschen-, dem sacktuch. blut, ein tüchtiger ratschen.

»wie die wüste gobi!» die bienen erwarten eine rekordernte. ein sausen,
ein sausen. nachts rast manchmal der ganze wald, rast Mnemosyne.

zerschlägt ihr zweibettzimmer, versucht's zumindest, reißt die letzten
dinge, das halbprivatzeug aus dem regal und von der wand. fotos.

wenn sie so weitermacht wird die stationsschwester für ein gitter-
bett sorgen müssen, fixierung. mit ihrer nachbarin, Mnemosyne II

ebenso verwirrt wie sie, hat sie verständnisschwierigkeiten. Mnemo-
syne wird fixiert, es sind erinnerungen: in kleinem atem summen

aneinander vorbei. die tage rasen. stille betten, in denen sie trocknen
wie die wüste gobi, und wollen nichts und wollen nicht vergehn.

von der stadt, malochend, die bienen. im bergwald steht seitlich ihr
wagen, der bienencontainer. lärchen in butter, ein summen unterm

lichtfilter, brausender punktierter baum, im sammelfuror der bienen
die einfluglöcher, schneisen, lichtüberspielten druckstellen, weich

gelber birnen. farbtafelhälfte des lärchwalds, um etwa diese jahreszeit.
so steht im bienengelb, wespenmäßig, ein angemischter, durchgeföhnter

gegenstand. ausschwärmende bestimmungsbücher, knatternde schatten
von seiten, darin der wind, die bö, sich zu schaffen macht. gegenstände

Bees, a Wasp

> nec miseros fallunt aconita legentes
> nor are the poor collectors fooled by monk's hood
> —Virgil, *Georgics*, Book II

with the hairline a mountain forest, that lets itself be heard.
mushroom gatherer, seeker in the dust of the foresters' road, who wanted to
tramp down into the valley: found

nothing: "dry as the gobi desert!" in the car he binds
his hand with handkerchief, sack-cloth. blood, a vigorous scratching

nothing: "as the gobi desert!" the bees expecting a record harvest. a humming,
a humming. at night the whole wood raves sometimes, Mnemosyne raves.

breaks up her two-bed room, tries at least, rips the last
things, the half private matter from the shelves and from the wall. photos.

if she goes on like that the ward sister will have to find
a bed with bars, fixing in place. Mnemosyne II

as confused as she is, has difficulties in understanding. Mnemo-
syne is fixed in place. they are memories: in a short breath humming

past each other. the days race. quiet beds, in which they dry like
the gobi desert, and want nothing and do not want to be past.

outside the town, grafting, the bees. in the mountain forest their car stands
aside, the bee transporter. larches in butter, a humming under the

light filter. splashing punched tree, in the bees' collecting delirium
the flying-in holes, rides, light-dappled dents of soft

yellow pears. colour scale half of larch wood, at about this time of year.
so a mixed, blow-dried object, wasplike, stands in the bee

yellow. books of foraging directions, crackling shadows
of pages in which the wind, the gust, makes itself busy. objects

stark an der lichtgrenze, zur schmerz-, zur baumgrenze hin. dort bauen sie
mohn an, schwankende fäuste, vor vögeln geschützt unter milchigem garn.

die machen an stangen sie mit wäscheklammern fest, allen, noch aus holz.
unterhalb, ein gutes stück weg, steht im halbschatten der bienen

container. mit den bunten einfluglöchern, jedes volk hat seinen eingang
abgestellt, in den grünen wald verbracht. da hingeknallt ihr karren. der

sucher: wie der gewinner beim R. M. Rilke-lookalike contest! stark über
frequentierte, gut bewachte löcher. das dichtervölkchen inspiriert:

communication blitz! sieht überwiegend aus wie (...)-write-alike-contest.
was spielt sich, forscher fragen, dahinter ab; da drinnen? es knistert

das antike stück, ein monstrum, deren X-ray-apparat. dies röntgen
schmeckt wie bienenstich. der dichter sitzt im strahlenkranz, was spielt

sich hinter deren schädelmasken ab, in triefen waben. bergkamm im haar-
ansatz, der imker trägt den gazekopf, verdrahtet, raucht die pfeife vor den

einfluglöchern, schneisen, taglichtüberspielt. druckstellen. druckstellen
gelber tafelbirnen, die, aufgeschnitten, schon besuch bekommen.

grundfarbe des papiers. grundfarbe des beschriebenen, zunotierten
ins wasser geflogenen papiers. verlaufsspuren, ränder, stadien der lesbarkeit.

die unlesbarkeitsstadien, stadien von papier. schauer und trocknungs-
prozess. lichtspielhauspapier, lichtspiel zimmer. wand und decke alles

vom bett aus gesehen. echt, das absolute!, dinge!, dolby super dings
da deren nadeln leuchten, zittern, trocknen und verklumpen. hitze

eine wespe. im zimmer, an die nachmittagsscheiben polternd, mit
dem wespenkopf, wieder und wieder. und wieder die schwester,

urlaubsreif; ein waldspaziergang schwebt vor ihr, birnenduft, die
schwester mit dem kaffee, wieder, mit der aufleuchtenden nadel.

tight on the light boundary. on the pain- on the tree boundary. there they
cultivate poppy, swaying fists, protected from birds under milky twine.

they fasten them to poles with clothes pegs, old ones, still wooden.
below, a good way away, in the half shadow stands the bee

transporter. with the coloured flying-holes. every swarm has its entrance.
set aside, taken to the green wood. there set their barrow down. the

seeker: like the winner in the R. M. Rilke look-alike contest! heavily over
used, well guarded holes. the poet swarm inspired:

communication blitz! looks overwhelmingly like a (…)write-alike contest.
what is going on, researchers ask, behind/ inside? the antique

piece creaks, a monster, their X-ray apparatus. this Röntgen
tastes like bee-sting. the poet sits in the wreath of rays, what is going

on behind their skull masks, in dripping combs. mountain ridge in the hair-
line, the beekeeper is carrying his gauze head, wired up, smokes his pipe before

the flying-in holes, rides, washed by daylight. dents. dents
of yellow dessert pears which, cut open, attract visitors.

ground colour of paper. ground colour of paper written on, noted on
flown into the water. flow courses, edges, stages of readability.

the stages of unreadability, stages of paper. shudder and drying
process. cinema paper, room for drama of light. wall and ceiling only

in sight of the bed. genuine, the absolute!, things! dolby super things
as their needles shine, tremble, dry and congeal. heat

a wasp. in the room, knocking against the afternoon panes, with
the wasp's head, again and again. and again the sister,

ready for leave; a walk in the woods is ready for her, scent of pears, the
sister with the coffee, again, with her brooch shining.

Der Schwarzwald 1932

> aber er mochte sein gedächtnis anstrengen,
> wie er wollte, weiter konnte er sich
> keines verses mehr entsinnen.
> Hauff, *Das kalte Herz* (1827)

eine strecke. wandernde sequenz.
und plötzlich werden diese bilder
und figuren jung *das stimmt nicht!*
um heftig sich sofort ins wort zu fallen—
als auferstehende, ein blick genügt,
ein blick genügt hier nicht,
was auf der einbildung beruht.

den mund vernäht der siebzigjährigen kinder (*fig.* 1),
die stürmisch maoam verlangen oder kinderüberraschung.
um, augenklappen später, umzusteigen auf rittersport und
fliegerschokolade. über dem kopf europas eine art hornissenbrausen;
in chören singen werden diese mädchen: weihnachtslieder, vor halben
männern zitternd angestimmt. dies sind die *folgenden figuren*: chor-
gesang vor kriegerwitwen auf der säuglingsstation.
das ist, über die alben hinaus,
voll stoff schwappend, überlaufend von stoff,
dies vielsprachige bilderzeug.
von dem, unfotografiert, jahrzehnte später noch
die reden gehen in familienresten.
stichworte über den stimmrest der toten,

tannenbühel, tannengruppen, hänge, tannenhorizonte;
vorm tannicht; steg aus tannenholz, auf dem
die kindergruppe hier posiert:

sander für arme!
fotos privat.
der schwarzwald 1932.

The Black Forest, 1932

> But strain his memory as he might,
> he could not call up any other line.
> —Hauff, *Das kalte Herz* (1827)

a spread. shuffle sequence.
and suddenly these pictures and figures
become young *that's not right!*
so as to quarrel with my own version, straight away
as resurrecting, a look is enough,
a look is not enough here,
which is based on imagination.

the sewn-up mouths of the 70-year old children (*fig.* 1)
who stormily demand fruity chews or childish surprise.
so as to, a bat of the eye later, convert to Rittersport
and aviation chocolate. above the head of europe a hornet buzzing;
these girls will sing in choirs: christmas carols, tremblingly
struck up before half men. these are the *following figures*: choral
song before war widows at the babies' ward.
that is, beyond the albums,
full of stuff spilling, overflowing with stuff,
this polylingual picture material.
about which, unphotographed, decades later
conversations in family remnants are still going.
key words about the remnant voice of the dead.

pine hills, pine groves, slopes, pine horizons;
before the pine cluster: path of pinewood, on which
the group of children is posed here:

Sander for the poor!
private collection photos
the Black Forest, 1932

fig. 2
ein totes material von abgestorbenen zellen stegen übergängen.
nadel, eher pipette, dieser dorfkirchtürme. der durch den raum
verholzte blick. dort hinter glatter grenze, diesig, eine weite
strecke, dort liegt basel; liegt die teure schweiz, verschwommen:
erasmus mit verformtem hinterschädel. hier: schwarzwaldkuppen.
soweit das auge reicht der kamera siehst grüne tannen du:
schwarzweiß.

fig. 4
ein aborigine in europas mitte, von *städters ethnoauge*
durch die kamera erfaßt: son hütejunge, alter circa zehn,
der hier mit stock und männerstrohhut, ohne schuh,
ins album aufgenommen wird. ein magerer cowboy,
übermüdet; den sechs stück fleckvieh stehn die knochen
ganz schön raus. die falle mißtrauen im trottenden auge.

sander für arme!
fotos privat.
der schwarzwald 1932.

eine fotostrecke, wandernde durchwandernde sequenz.
die tannenhochformate. und plötzlich werden diese
bildertiere und figuren wieder jung *das stimmt nicht*
um sich sofort ins wort zu fallen als auferstehende,
ein blick genügt. *stimmt nicht stimmt nicht stimmt*
die mageren sind die platzenden alben.

gewilderte strecke. die schwarzwaldexpedition im jahre 1932.
legendäre legende aus geländern, schluchten, unebenheiten
im körper der gelände; die tannenstillen oder -stimmen.
querformate, in größtmöglicher auflösung begriffen.
wir haben zweiunddreißig binnen kurzem
alle möglichkeiten *das stimmt.*

die expeditionsfotografin stellt scharf.
           die toten amateure, schwarzweiß,
wie die lebenden (überlebenden), bilden die gefälschte

fig. 2
a dead material of died-off cells paths crossings.
needle, more likely a pipette, of these village church towers. the gaze
turned to wood by the space. there behind flat border, misty, a far
stretch, over there is Basel; lies precious Switzerland, blurred:
Erasmus with deformed occiput. here: black forest treetops.
as far as the camera's eye reaches you see green pines:
black and white.

fig. 4
an aboriginal in the middle of Europe, grasped by *townie's*
ethno-eye through the camera: it's a shepherd boy, age about ten,
who here with crook and man's straw hat, no shoes,
is received into the album. a thin cowboy,
overtired; the ten head of cattle with patches have bones that
stick out quite neatly. mistrust of a trap in the slowly lumbering eye.

Sander for the poor!
photos private collection.
the Black Forest, 1932

a spread of photos. shuffle sequence, flicking through.
the pines in portrait format. and suddenly these
picture animals and figures become young *that's not right*
so as to quarrel with my version, straight away,
as resurrecting, a look is enough. *that's not right not right not*
the thin ones are the bursting albums.

poached spread. the black forest expedition of the year 1932.
legendary legend made of terrains, ravines, unevennesses
in the body of the terrain; the pine-stillnesses or -voices.
landscape format, caught with maximum resolution.
we will soon have thirty-two
all possibilities *that's right.*

the expedition's female photographer focuses.
                    the dead amateurs, black and white,
as the living (surviving), form the faked

strecke. tannen starren, menschen erstarren im moment.
momentaufnahmen von fotogruppen.
keins der kinder,
die sich fremd sind, blickt ins bild.
zurücklegen oder -lehnen ist nicht möglich, was solls.

fig. 5
sieh diese strecke: in einmachgläsern, zuckend, präparate
der geschichte. liegt etwa deutschlands herz hier, tanzend?
hier in aller fotoalben? genau beschriftet alle exponate.
und nächster versuch, die nächste figur. wir wechseln,
ein moment nur, mal eben hier die namen und die
daten aus. zum beispiel *(folgt zitat über mexik. fotograf)*

oder aber: während tannenstimmen rauschen, blicken
augen aus kaurischnecken aus den menschenköpfen
der museen. aus den fotos, fotostrecken, weit entfernt.
der hütejunge zieht den hut – tief ins gesicht.
weit in die böden eingesackte ahnenkörper.

das sind mitbringsel nur. die keinem, der jetzt lebt
von der familie etwas sagen (zucken). kopfsouvenire. *das stimmt
nicht.* urlaub in der vorzeit. sind etwa dies die schwarzwaldköpfe?
städter, die gesichtsschädel ausmodelliert? städteraugen die bilder?
echthaarperücken aus staub?

zuckender strahl, erneutes blitzlicht. und innenaufnahme: ein kranium,
als trinkschale. der hütejunge zieht den hut. hier wurden weisenköpfe
unterm fußboden (aus tannenholz) vergraben. bis hierhin reicht nicht
mißgebildetes licht; es werden davon fotos aufgenommen.

sander für arme.
fotos privat.
der schwarzwald 1932.

gedicht ist immer ahnenstrecke. fotostrecke, angereichert und,
ganz klar: gefälscht. wodurch die ahnenstrecke wahr wird erst.
gedicht ist schaltung;
reportage klang, die meerzahnschnecke gibt dem auge biß.

spread. pines stare, humans freeze up in the moment.
momentary snaps of photo groups.
none of the children,
who are strange to themselves, is looking into the lens.
lying back or leaning back is not possible, so what.

fig. 5
see this spread: in fruit jars, twitching, specimens
of history. does Germany's heart lie here, dancing?
here in all the photo albums? all the exhibits precisely labelled.
and next experiment, next figure, we switch,
just a moment, here the names and the
dates. for example *(quote on mexico follows. photographer)*

or again: while pine voices rustle, eyes
gaze out of cowry shells out of the human heads
of the museums. from the photos, spreads of photos, far distant.
the shepherd lad pulls his hat – down onto his face.
ancestor bodies sagged deep into the earths.

these are just what we brought home. that say nothing to
anyone still alive in the family (twitch). souvenir heads. *that's
not right.* holiday in the primitive. so are these the black forest heads?
a townie, who is modelling skull faces? the pictures town eyes?
real hair wigs made of dust?

jerking beam, renewed flash on. and interior shot: a cranium
as drinking bowl. the shepherd lad pulls his hat off. here wise heads
were buried under the soil (of pinewood). malformed
light does not reach as far as this; photos were taken of it.

Sander for the poor.
private photos.
the Black Forest, 1932

poem is always spread of ancestors. photo spread, enriched and,
really clear: faked. through which the ancestor spread first becomes true.
poem is switching;
sound reportage, the tusk shell gives the eye its bite.

nimm diesen dort; in knickerbockern, ein studienrat von
sechsundvierzig jahren.
vor sechs jahren MEIN KAMPF gelesen: *wenn dieser mann*
an die regierung kommt, gibt es krieg für ganz europa.

skeptiker mit wanderstock,
über engel: über der landschaft, über verwesenden.
der himmel – eine speichelprobe.
verwesende engel. über verwesende engel, versteht sich;

es tut mir leid: gedicht ist nun einmal: schädelmagie.

take that one there: in knickerbockers, a senior teacher
of age forty-six.
six years ago read MEIN KAMPF: *if this man
comes into the government, there will be war for the whole of Europe.*

sceptic with walking-stick,
about angels: about the landscape, about decaying things.
heaven – a saliva test.
decaying angels. about decaying angels, naturally;

I am sorry: poem is finally: skull magic.

Larven

1913 sind auf Papua-Neuguinea die ströme und
gebirge längst nach den Hohenzollern benannt.

der kopf der fremde schnurrt und liefert. für neue
ferne dinge neue namen wobei die sprachn sich

vermischen. im mund der fremdes neues schmeckt
wie kopra oder kasuar. das paßt zum helm. so

dampfen neue masken aus den sumpf-eiländern
auf die feierliche zunge abendland. die gaumen

segel knattern frisch ein wind aus übersee. berlin –
die zunge – erhebt als frische toteninsel sich aus

dem fiebersumpf der mark. die insel schnalzt schon
kommen worte aus der ferne. südfrüchte fallen

der stadt aus dem mund. der ist die neue zunge so
gesprächig. anders irgendwie: es sprechen alle plötzlich

wie die papuas, hofsprache iatmul. der mund als über-
see, als schein. so strömt der sepik mündet in den rhein.

Ghosts

in 1913 the rivers and mountains on Papua New Guinea
have long since been named after Hohenzollerns.

the head of the alien whirrs and delivers. for new
faraway things new names as languages

mix. in the mouth which savours the alien the new
like copra or cassowary. that goes with the helmet. so

new masks from the swamp-islands steam
on the sublime tongue of the Westland. the palates

billow crackle with a fresh wind from overseas. berlin –
the tongue – raises itself as a fresh island of the dead out

of the fever swamp of the March. the island clicks its tongue already
words are coming out of the faraway. tropical fruits fall

from the town's mouth. whose new tongue is so
chatty. somehow other: suddenly everyone

is speaking like the Papua, court language Iatmul. the mouth as over-
sea, as appearance. so the Sepik flows and runs into the Rhine.

Paläolaryngologie – Alte Kehlen

zielfoto. schuß, gegenschuß. das wild, bejagt, das durchs bild
springt, durch bilder, durch bildsavannen, über ebenen, ja: hoch-

ebenen, niederungen, feuchtgebiete, plattland, über rest-
sumpf sich fort zu machen wünscht. *es genügt ein geräusch,*

dentaler pirschwink. gewöhnliches röhricht, das kommuniziert.
der kehlkopf ist es, der sich bewegt, schluckbewegungen, jäger.

in bewegung befinden sich die bänder und sehnen. es ist dies
wild ihre target-group. das sich abmacht, in die büsche schlägt.

pfeile, immer den pfeilen nach, dem pfiff um die ecke. da sucht,
während sprachen kleine sprachen werden und verschwinden,

was, in bockigem dahineilen, sich zu entziehn. in einiger weite
entferntes zungenbein, zungenbeginn: *die gezähmte felskürzel.*

augenprojektile, flackerndes ohr, das werkzeug schnellt ab, nenn,
nennenswerte geschwindigkeiten werden erreicht, was für prä-

zisionen! hand in hand beschnitzte kranien, schädel mit gebrauchs-
spuren, hohlkörper, schöpfkelle. text dazu. das alles geht von

hand zu hand, nicht unbedingt in jede. nicht an jedem scheiß
stein oder überhängen, in den wänden gabelsberger. schwer zu-

gänglich die steige, die stellen, die abschnellende, wegflit-
schende dinge angekrakelt sind. hier sind rechnungen offen. ein

falsches wort! ressourcen, umkämpfte quellen, nebst kalendar
systemen. uhren und mondkalender. minimales

raschel-raschel, ein knacks von trocknem rohr, *ein geräusch,* und
es wird so was wie präzision, wie sprachgeschwindigkeit erreicht.

Palaeolaryngology — Ancient Throats

photo of target. shot, counter shot. the game, hunted, jumping through the
picture, through pictures, through pictured savannahs, over plains, yes: high

plains, depressions, wetlands, flatlands, over undrained
swamp, it wants to get away. *one sound is enough*

dental stalk signal. usual reed thicket, that communicates.
it is the larynx which moves, swallowing sounds, hunters.

the tendons and sinews are in movement. this game is
their target-group. it makes off, speeds into the bushes.

arrows, after the arrows, the whistle round the corner. there something,
while languages become dwindling languages and disappear,

tries to withdraw in headstrong haste. at a distance
detached tongue bone, tongue begin: *the tamed rock abbreviation.*

eye projectiles, quivering ear, the implement launches. mem,
memorable speeds are attained, such pre-

cisions! hand in hand carved cranium, skull with traces
of wear, hollow body, scoop. text on that. all that goes

from hand to hand, not always to every one. not to every shit
stone or overhang, in the walls of pitman's. difficult of

access the hill path, the places where startling, fleeting
away things are scrawled. here accounts are open. a

wrong word! resources, disputed sources, beside calendar
systems. clocks and moon records. minimal

rustle-rustle, crack of a dry reed, *one sound*, and
such a thing as precision, as speed of speech, is reached.

bildprogramme

1
zwischnbericht

gegnüber. eingelassene plattn; pro-
tzigste heraldik. weißestn marmors
parade: di superfette SPRACH-
INSTALLATION.

        (innenan-
sicht außnvor hat sichsn fürstbi-
schof feingemacht, getäfelt, drin, drauf-
sicht intarsienspielchn; draufsicht turm-
ofn ALLEGORIEN; nix wi mädels
mit blankn möpsn auffe reliefkacheln,
hübsch glasierte ofnwärme.)

                        und vor-
geblendet. kellen, kehrbleche. aus-
gräbersound. DIE GESCHICHTE
HERBRETTERND AUF SACKKARREN.
der ganze weggeächzte schutt, durch-
gesiebte sprache. dies asservieren auf
knien; kratzen geschieht, gekratz, bürstn,
abgepinselt. knien, nebenander, an
irgend (kloster)mauer bei rasselndm,
heiser schlürfendm INDUSTRIESTAUB
SAUGER. so landn, schürf-schürf, schä-
del in obstkistn marke »papa clemente«;
säuberlich schädeldeckn (caput mortuum),
sargbrettchn (pestbeständig, siena) in
cellophantütn, auf geflattertm, windgezerr-
tm zeitungspapier. gotisch und durch-
numeriert. durchnumerierter
grabungsbericht.

instructions to a painter

1
interim report

opposite, inlaid slabs; most
cocky heraldry. parade of whitest
marble: the super-fat SPEECH-
INSTALLATION.
                    (interior-
view front and outside: has dressed up
his prince-bishop, clad in wood, inside. over-
view intarsia puzzles; overview tower-
oven ALLEGORIES; nothing but girls
with shining pugs on the relief tiles,
prettily glazed oven warmth.)
                                and super-
imposed to front. ladles, metal trays. ex-
cavator sound. TRUNDLING HISTORY UP
ON WHEELBARROWS.
the whole debris creaking away, sieved
speech. curating this
on knees; scratching happening, process of scratch, brushing,
with fine hairs. kneeling, side by side, at
some (cloister) wall with a rattling,
hoarsely slurping INDUSTRIAL
VACUUM CLEANER. so land, scrape-scrape, skulls
in fruit boxes brand "papa clemente";
cleanly skull roofs (caput mortuum),
coffin planks (plague holding, siena) in
cellophane bags, on fluttering, wind-
tugged newspaper. gothic and serial
numbered. serially numbered
excavation report.

2

mitschnitt calvenschlacht

inzwischn: 1499. luftbilder, -spiegel,
spiegelungn ausm engadinerkrieg. ein
sommerlicher brückenkopp (gesprengt) so
nimmt das wasser andre farbe an.
                                    di gute
geschoßverschraubte luft! im luftzug
NAPALMHEIDE / das in den fluß
zischt, nähte zwischen leib und panzern
zieht (»da ist ja keine landschaft mehr«,
TONLOS / »hättns sollen fahren
lassn«). darüber geht di kamera, ho-
lpernd; kamerafahrt heiser, angekro-
chenes aug. vorm ortler. vor schi-
mmerndn 3000ern: demolirte sand-
sackberge (...)
              und sorgnfaltn, kummer-
volles redaktörsgesic't: ICH HÖRE EBEN!,
ICH RUFE WILLIBALD PIRKHEIMER
(sonst in Nürnberg stationiert!), am sattel, AM HU-
MANISTISCHEN SATTELLITTNTELEPHON:

PIRKHEIMER: ja, hier pirkheimer. humanitär-
sanitäre verhältnisse ... mit grawenvollen bildern
zu tun ... habn hohe-luste zu zeichnen ... di
geiselerschießung von meran ... (FADING),
obwohl bevölkerun' dagegn ... (RAUSCH-
RAUSCH), im -iegesrausch, durchrau-
schende flüchtlinge ... strom weg, alles weg ...
KAISER MAXIMILIAN SOLL GEWEINT
HABN ALS / FADING /DI KINDER ESSENZ /
BROTKLEE VON DEN WIESN da br-
                                    icht
di leitun' zamm, damundherrn, in weißm rau-
schn, klappt zusamm das bilderwelt in riesen OH-
NELÖSCHLÖSCH. romanisch di bandnwerbun'
Gottes, tonlos di engel vorm himml. jerusalem, wei-
ße bänder spruchbänder in händn. ohne text.

2
live recording Battle of Chalavaina

meanwhile: 1499. aerial shots, fata morganas,
mirages from the engadine war. a
summertime bridgehead (routed) so
the water takes on a different colour.
                                    the good
shell-screwed air! in the draft
NAPALMHEATH / that falls
hissing into the river, draws seams between body and
armour ("there isn't any landscape any more",
SOUNDLESS / "should have let it
go"). the camera goes over it, lim-
ping; hoarse camera track, eye crawl-
ling up. before the ortler. before shim-
mering 3000 meter peaks: demolished sand-
bag mounds (…)
                        and care lines, worried
editor face: I AM NOW HEARING,
I AM CALLING WILLIBALD PIRKHEIMER
(normally stationed in Nuremberg!), in the saddle, on the HU-
MANISTIC SATELLITE PHONE:

PIRKHEIMER: yes, pirkheimer here. humanitarian-
sanitary conditions … footage which doth us to Grue
… notching up heavy losses … the
hostage shooting of meran … (FADING),
although in contrast population … (HISS-
HISS), in -ictory thrill, streams of
refugees … power down, everything down…
KAISER MAXIMILIAN SAID TO HAVE WEPT
HAVE AS / FADEOUT / THE CHILDREN EATING /
FENUGREEK FROM THE MEADOWS the conn-
                                            ection
breaks off, ladies and gentlemen, in white
hiss, the picture world closes up in wooden chutes ERASE? NOT
ERASE. romanesque the ads for god
along the stadium walls, soundless the angels before the heavenly
Jerusalem, white captions speaking captions in hands. without text.

3
streifnhintergründe

        als stünde
dem schlüsselmann, blitzeblau,
die bergfarbe im haar:
        hochzüng-,
höchstzüngelnder lapislazuli [1] in
kopfüberducktm tibet. gewölbejoch
gewölbefeld, gewölbter scheitel,
in tagwerkn gemessener farb-
auftrag. WIR STREIFEN
GERADE MAL DIE HINTER
GRÜNDE / feuchtigkeitsein-
brüche; ein liegn auf haupthöhe.
befallne passi, paßhöhen be-
nannt, benommen und FEINPUTZ /
ORIGINALPUTZ gesagt, oder
meerpalme, zu klammem material,
schreibmaterie hingebeugter chro-
nist: zeitmenschen in wallun', in wand-
lun' begriffn (oberstübchens skriptorium).
der blick der di wandfelder begattet: der
westwand der südtrepps dem ostseite zur
nordkappe. lippmlesend dies.
lippmlesn. strahl.

[1]: *aufgeriebener lasurstein mit*
10 bis 30 µ großn körnern.

3
painting backgrounds

                                         as if
the colour of the mountain, lightning blue,
was in the keyholder's hair:
                             high-dart-
highest flickering lapis lazuli [1] in
head-ducking Tibet. domed col
domed field, curved apex.
colour application measured
in work days. WE ARE JUST
PAINTING THE BACK
GROUNDS / invasions of
moisture; lying down at head height…
damaged passages, heights of passes
named, weakened and FINE DECORATION
ORIGINAL DECORATION said, or
pillow coral, over damp material,
writing material chron-
icler stooping: contemporaries caught up in turmoil,
in transit (small upper room's scriptorium).
the look which begets the mural fields: of the
west wall of the south staircase of the east side to the
north cowling. lip-reading this.
lip-reading. beam.

[1] *ground-up glaze stone with
10 to 30 μ grains.*

Pieter Bruegel: alchemie headset

gebrau, ich mein, gebrauch,
der erschließt sich in fragen.
folgen der zungen,
der zangenbewegung.
                              in affenhitze
wälzer und zettel. rezepte und kram.
labormitschrift, post it, zutat beschriftet.
texte auf säcken, halbfertiges. rohmaterial.
schon
                                        rutscht
dem die kappe, nicken genügt – sichtschutzmässig
über die augn; sitzt ganz gebeugt da –
                                  mit säuren
hantiert wird, feuer mal aus und mal aus-
schlägt; entzündliches, fingerndes, fremdes
gezüngel. leicht brennbar, halt drauf jetzt;
das alles

in diesem ... wie sagt man? labor doch wohl kaum.
bruchbude, bruchbuden-klima. der kehrt uns
den rücken. wir kriegen den seitlich. belegschaft
am machn. das sieht man:
die leute
sind unterbezahlt.

anweisung rechts
von dem lesepult aus. gebrauchsgegenstände,
kram-katarakt:
ein kleben, ein knirschen unter den sohlen,
ein siff rechts und links, echtes chaos.
das ganze von teilen und teilchen
übern sprachraum verteilt.

heillos! doch
voll brennbar die atmo.

Pieter Brueghel: alchemy headset

cussed, I mean, custom,
that explains itself in questions.
sequences of tongues,
of tong movements.
      in apelike heat
old tomes and paper slips. recipes and clutter.
laboratory record, post its, ingredient written on.
texts in sacks, half finished. raw material.
already
        his cap
is slipping, a nod is enough – like goggles
over the eyes; sits quite stooped there –
         fiddling
with acids, fires out or break
out; infectious, fingering, foreign
flickers. easily flammable, stop it now;
all that

in this ... call it what? laboratory will hardly do.
condemned shack, condemned shack feeling. it turns
its back on us. we get it sideways. staff
in the making. you can see:
the staff
are underpaid.

directions on the right
of the reading desk. objects for use,
cataract of clutter:
sticky, grinding under the soles,
a mess right and left, genuine chaos.
the ensemble divided in parts
and particles over the linguistic field.

insoluble! but
the atmosphere fully flammable.

kelle und becken. siebe, pipette.
ich mein: brauchbares blasenschlagen. schneiden und rühren;
aussieben, mixen. am ausköcheln vorne die irgendwie
was! aus leder ein ächzen: blasebalg-set: einer am ruhen und
einer in betrieb.

jetzt assistentin.
auch voll am machen, auch schon was älter.
lässig und wissend, blick in die linse.

pult. pizzaverpackung.
auch ganz belagert,
das ist doch hier echter
scharteken-wust!
foliantenbelagert,
wust von fingerzeigen,
chaotisches chaos
von staubigen files!

tritt da nich drauf! mensch, reiß
da nix runter! die hitze. das hält doch
nun wirklich keiner drin aus.

die flaschen. krüge und tiegel und trichter.
in mörsernder hitze blinde phiolen. fenster
geöffnet und fensterbild-ausblick. es hilft nichts
gegen die scharfen gerüche, luft bleibt zum
schneiden. zischeln und zischen von unausgesetzt
simmernder köchelei.

die ablage drüben? auch
improvisiert, klar. da hamse die waage,
mal schnell abgelegt, drogistenwerkzeug
liegt übereck liegt das; die eine der schalen
voll nußgroßer bröckchen; da sind doch
nicht etwa nuggets dabei?

ALPHATIER. das alphatier als bunter
hund, so lesen wir, entziffern was wie
ERDSCHRIFT, ZEPHIRE

scoop and basin. sieves, pipettes.
I mean: usable bubble beater. cut and stir;
sift out, shake together. gently simmering down up front the somehow
something! a creaking from leather: bellows set: one resting and
one at work.

        now female assistant.
also fully engaged, also a bit older.
relaxed and knowing, look into the lens.

desk. pizza packing.
even quite surrounded,
this is just a genuine
rubble of calfskins!
besieged by folios,
rubble of bookmarks,
chaotic chaos
of dusty files!

don't tread on anything! no, don't
pull anything down! the heat. really no-one
can stand it in there.

the bottles. jugs and troughs and funnels.
blind vials in pulverising heat. windows
opened and the view through windows. nothing helps
with the acrid smells, the air stays
thick to cut. whistling and hissing of incessantly
simmering low cooking.

the rack over there? also
improvised, clearly, they've just tidied
the scales away quickly, druggist's apparatus
lying canted on edge lying; one of the bowls
full of clumps the size of nuts; there wouldn't
be any nuggets in there?

ALPHA ANIMAL. the alpha animal as dog everyone
knows, we read. decipher something like
EARTH SCRIPT, ZEPHYRS

was über die böden so schwappt und —
so kippt — wer
das schon wissen will? lies weiter. lies

ALPHATIER, ERDSCHRIFT-ZEPHIRE,
ALGHE MIST lies
alles umsonst

zum lachen. dem fällt,
geduckt vor erregung,
im sprung der,
der schlappen gleich ab.

what is swashing and tipping
over the floors — who
actually wants to know that? read on. read

ALPHA ANIMAL. EARTH SCRIPT- ZEPHYRS.
ALGHE MIST read
all in vain

laughably. whose
stooping with excitement,
in mid leap he,
slipper just slips off.

UNBEKANNT, auf welchem
konzil sie geradewegs

verboten: die schreinmadonna.
im aufklappbaren im aufgeklappten

bauchraum: darstellung der dreifältigkeit.
und haben für immer der ihren bauch

mit kräftigen nägeln der ihren bauch
für immer vernäht. eisen die

ins lindenholz geglitten sind. aus linden
holz die ewige herren welt – weiß

keiner wo die abgeblieben ist.
die mutter mit der kräftigen nase mit

dem balancierenden mit dem auf ihrem
schenkel balancehaltenden kind haben sie

dann vergessen oder ausrangiert (gotik)
irgendwann wieder gefunden in einem

pfarrhauswinkel. original ins museum und
zur versicherung ein duplikat gemacht.

natürlich nicht zum aufklappen also ohne
bauchraum ohne einbruchsbecken ohne nägel

ohne die verwitterungen im holz. ohne
kerben einrisse zertalungen ohne herzcanyon

tiefste vertiefung verlaufspur und talgrund
sieht aber gut aus. keine frage gut gemacht.

UNKNOWN, at which
Council she was expressly

forbidden: the Madonna of the shrine.
in the openable, in the opened

belly of the box: image of the trinity.
and have forever her belly

with strong nails her belly
forever stitched up. irons which

have slid into the limewood. of lime
wood the lord's eternal world – no-one

knows where that one is lurking.
the mother with the powerful nose with

the balancing with the on her
hip balance-holding child they have

then forgotten or put in storage (gothic era)
someday rediscovered in the ingle

of a vicarage. original to the museum and
a duplicate made for safety.

naturally not operable so without
belly space without collapse craters without nails

without the wear in the wood. without
notches tears grooves without heart-canyon

deepest scores drip trail and flow course
but looks good. well made no question.

Der Similaun. Director's Cut

gewitterblaue tattoos.
in *dr. camcorder's* alpiner
bilderklinik bereitet man
die not-op inzwischen vor.

die berge als silexspitzen, als
Similaun-fragment. geschickte
aufnahmen nach dem leben.
die berge als schulterblätter.

als pfannen und kugeln, die
berge die berge als kugelgelenk,
die schmelzwässer, die schmerz-
wässer. silexgebirge in der schulter

und weiße gelenkpfannen:
aufnahmen, notaufnahmen.
kettenreaktion im freeze, darüber,
auskugelnd, die sonne rollt.

abnahm der hirt den hut;
tat ihn ab als er nach wochen
über steilhänge, vom gipfel
aus; holzscheiben in brand,

schweifziehende feuer. serien
von flammen und dia-serien,
serien flackernder stills zischend
zu tal geschleudert: den *sicht-*

zwang erregend in keuchender
luft. dies die befunde.
camcorder läßt sich inzwischen
birkenporling reichen.

The Similaun. Director's Cut

storm blue tattoos.
meanwhile in *dr. camcorder's*
alpine picture clinic they are
preparing the emergency operation.

the mountains as silex points, as
Similaun-fragment. skilled
photos taken from life.
the mountains as shoulderblades.

as sockets and balls, the
mountains the mountains as ball joint.
the meltwaters, the pain-
waters. silex mountains in the shoulder

and white joint sockets:
exposures, emergency shelters.
chain reaction in freezeframe, over which,
wrenched, the sun rolls.

the shepherd took down the hut;
hid it when after weeks he,
over steep slopes, starting
from the peak; wooden discs in the fire,

tail-trailing fire. series
of flames and slide-series,
series of flickering stills hurled
hissing downhill: *optic*

compulsion aroused in panting
air. this the results.
camcorder has meanwhile
the birch fungus handed to him.

birkenporling stillt das blut,
desinfiziert die wunde.
als nach wochen gefragt,
gefragt wurde, der hirte,

ob zusammen ein foto
gemacht werden könnte?
eine sichtmuren-auslösung,
wespen in der luft oder

silex. grasmantel, das ausgeschälte
licht und freigelegte bastfaser.
grasmantel, alpine kotze (cotton)
aus süssgras. die zwirnbindung.

im regelmäß grasschnüre an-
geknotet: *unklare funktion*
mit den händen hält der hirt
den hut auf seinem schoss,

die haare, wie er nachfühlt,
liegen richtig. sanderblick.
und lernten von sprache. lernten
den wespeneingang kennen

unter der schuppentür.
leicht unter dem Similaun,
befundlos vor kodaks tiefe.
dort, und am knie, hier:

tattoos von gewitterbläue.
verstopfte gefäße. hier ist der
eingang, leicht zu übersehn: »da
sind ja wespen!«, »weiß schon«

nun aber, da klarstes wasser
im rücken, von gletschermilch
trüb überspült die krümmung
betrifft. nu, als silex, die silex-

the fungus staunches the bleeding,
disinfects the wound.
when after weeks they asked,
asked, the shepherd,

if they could be
in a photo together?
releasing a glacial torrent of sight,
wasps in the air or

silex. grass cloak, the hollowed out
light and stripped bark fibres.
grass cloak, alpine plaid (cotton)
from sweet grass. the twine ligature.

uniform length grass laces strung
on: *function unclear.*
with his hands the shepherd
holds his hat on his lap,

his hair, as he checks,
lying right. Sander gaze.
and learnt from speech. learnt
how to know the wasps' entrance

under the door of scales.
slightly under the Similaun,
without results before a kodak's depth.
there, and on the knee, here:

tattoos of storm blue.
blocked vessels. here is the
entrance, easy to miss: "there
are wasps!", "know already"

now though, as clearest water
at his back, dully overwashed
by glacier milk which concerns the
gradient. now, when silex, the silex-

spitze in dem sein rücken eintritt
und glatte zehn jahre später erst
herausgeröntgt wird, und er sich
legen mußte und hingreift, zu-

drückt, den schmerz zu dämmen,
in der tiefe der schulter; er sich
zusammenzuhalten versucht
einige zeit noch, klamm.
dann
kältegebiet.
der berge
zottiger grauwert.

point entered his back
and ten whole years later
it shows up in X-ray, and he had
to lay down and grips,

presses, to stem the pain,
in the depth of the shoulder; he tries
to hold himself together
a while longer, chilled.
then
the region of cold.
the shaggy
greyscale
of the mountains.

Bärengesang

I

Ich kannte dreizehn worte
für mein bein,
für meinen fuß,
für bärenbein und bärenfuß.
die kenn ich nun nicht mehr.

Elf worte für mein auge
so sagt' ich zu ihm; stern
zu meinem
bärenauge.
die kenn ich nun nicht mehr.

Mit dem leichten hintern
des hasenmännchens
sprangen wir vom boot an land,
zahlreich wir, männer und frauen.
sahen die hagebutteninsel.

Vernahmen die rote,
die hagebuttennachricht –
so groß so prall wie rentierlippen.
eine eisenkette, klirrend, aus
licht, die herabhing vom himmel.

Vom siebenschlündigen himmel:
herabhing, klirrend, wie silber,
mich aufzunehmen, aufstieg:
nach meinem bärentod, dem bären-
fest, dem -tanz.

Bear Song

I

I knew thirteen words
for my leg
for my foot,
for bearleg and bearfoot.
I can't remember them any more.

Eleven words for my eye
so I said to him: star
to my
bear eye.
I can't remember them any more.

With the light rear
of the hare man
we leapt from the boat to the shore,
being numerous, man and women,.
saw the island of haw berries.

Heard the red,
the haw berry information –
so big so full as reindeer lips.
an iron chain, clinking,
made of light, hung down from the sky.

From the seven-throated sky:
hung down, clinking, like silver,
to take me up, climbed up:
after my bear-death, the bear-
feast, the -dance.

II

Dieser ostjakische…, dies
die zusammenlegbare nachricht.
über die zarten bühel
übern permafrost hell meterdick
und's dickicht, gutgelaunte bödn.

Überm mammut-hort drobm
die sonne als faulbeerreichtum
glatt-erstrahlend!
der mond verdeckt halb
als freche hagebutte!

Die hagebutteninsel über
und über gedeckt – rotphase.
schrift abkeknickter ästchen.
ein mischwald, ein birkigt,
erschillernder lindenhain.

Der ahlbeerkirsche zusammen-
legbare nachricht: da sprangen zahl-
reiche männer und frauen, bärenherzig,
mit den leichten hintern der hasen
aus dem vogelgeschmückten ans

Ufer, aus scharfnasigem boot.
ich kannte acht worte für meine
eingeweide, für meine galle
für bäreneingeweid, für bärengalle.
die kenn ich nun nicht mehr.

III

Ziehen über jägersteige
steif, in abrutschendem dampf.
und ziehen aus den köchern,
während die hunde wittern: die
zweispitzign, die pfeile heraus.

II

This Ostyak…, this
the composable information.
over the delicate hillocks
over the permafrost bright metre-thick
and the thicket, good-tempered soils.

Over the mammoth-shelter up there
the sun as dead-berry-wealth
smoothly shining!
the moon half concealed
as a cheeky haw berry!

The haw berry island covered
over and over – red phase.
script of bent back twigs
a mixed forest, a birch stand,
shimmering lime grove.

The spike-berry cherry's compos-
able information: then numerous
men and women leapt, bear-hearted,
with the light rear of the hares
out of the bird-decorated to the

Shore, out of sharp-nosed boat.
I knew eight words for my
insides, for my gall
for bear insides, for bear gall.
I can't remember them any more.

III

Draw over hunter's rise
stiff, in steam sliding down.
and draw out of the quivers,
as the hounds scent: the
two-pointed, the arrows, out.

Wo sie beeren rauften: schrie! ich
sie an aus vollem hals gleich einem:
bärenwaldtier, und sie floh'n. doch
eins erwischt' ich, deren mutter wie ein
fohlen mir zu ehren hatte noch getanzt.

»Armes mädchen, du bist tot, du bist tot!«
vor todenangst schon tot, so rief ich, warf
ich sie in meinen hohlen, zahnvollen mund.
in meinen bärenmund und ich benagte es,
das mädchen – als wenn's ein entlein wär.

Mit pfeilen, mit dem riemenspeer,
zuletzt dem eisenbeil, mit seines rückens
stumpfem gegenstand, so drangen sie
umzingelnd auf mich ein – ach, rotphase.
                    so starb den Großen Tod des

Bären-ich – sie nahmen mir
den heiligen, den unversehrten pelz.
wie wenn der elster man die haut
abzieht! dann bärengasterei.
gefolgt vom bärentanz.

Worauf der himmelsmann
– mein siebenschlündiger vater –
an klirrender eisenkette, die wie
reines silber klang: mich nach oben
zog, mich: im silberschmuck!

Ich kannte alle worte
für kralle, magen, mund und kopf.
für bärenkralle, bärenmagen,
bärenzungenspitze,
für meinen bärenkopf.

die kenn ich nun nicht mehr.
die brauch ich nun nicht mehr.

(für Heidi Kling, 1927-2005)

Where they plucked berries: shouted! I
at them from full throat like a:
bear wood creature, and they fled. but
I caught one, whose mother had
in my honour been dancing like a foal.

"Poor maiden, you are dead, you are dead!"
dead just from fear of death, I called, threw
her into my hollow, teeth-filled mouth.
into my bear mouth and I gnawed it,
the girl – as if it were a duckling.

With arrows, with the spear thrower,
finally the iron axe, with the
blunt object of its back, so they pressed
around me encircling – oh, red phase.
                    so died the Great Death

Of the Bear-me – they took from me
my holy, my undamaged skin.
as when one pulls the pelt off
a jackdaw! then bear hospitality,
followed by the bear dance.

At which the sky man
– my seven-throated father –
on clinking iron chain, that rang
like pure silver: drew me upwards,
me: in the silver array!

I knew all the words
for claw, stomach, mouth and head.
for bear claw, bear stomach,
bear tongue tip,
for my bear head.

I don't know them any more.
I don't need them any more.

(for Heidi Kling, 1927-2005)

Die Himmelsscheibe von Nebra I

          Nach
nordnordwesten zu
da liegt ein brocken
mir im blick.
blickbrocken.
gesplittertes bild.
den sehen, sehen wir
vom erdwerk aus,
im horizont.
          den sehen,
den fixieren sie
vom erdwerk aus: bei klarer luft
und festem datum.

          sind irgend feiern das,
mit ausgefeilter lichtregie –
ich weiß es nicht, und darf das auch
nicht wissen,
von denen wir
nichts wissen dürfen.
(erdwerk schürfen).

und nur die palisade ahmt den zahnstand nach.

The Sky Disc of Nebra I

                        Towards
north-northwest
there lies a clump
before my sight.
sightclump.
splinter picture.
that we see, see
from on the earthwork,
in the horizon.
                      that they see,
that they fix
from on the earthwork: on a clear day
and a set date.

                are those some kind of ceremonies
with refined light-design –
I don't know, and neither am allowed
to know,
of which we are allowed
to know nothing.
(burrow an earthwork)

and only the palisade imitates the setting of cogs.

Die Himmelsscheibe von Nebra — Epilog

Unter wolknschluck-
                    hortfunde, gesichelt,
während der bodn murrt.
                    die vielen
aufblendungen darin,

die: in vielfach ab-
geblendeter gegnd.

unter wolkenschluckauf
dies:
Murnau'sche jagen,
lauthals vielleicht,
halb augnlos,
in aufgeblendeter und
                    wieder
abgeblendeter gegnd:
                    Murnaus
                    wilde schattenjagd.
                                        so
geht die gegnd, so gehtse in fetzn —

unter vielen weißblenden,
und blitzbildern.

steady cam, murrend.

ja.
tcha.

da ist progredienz drin.
im murrenden, im muckenden
organ.
        schattenmeldung, die
sich in den
gehörgang stürzt, nicht licht-

The Sky Disc of Nebra – Epilogue

Under cloudswallow-
                           hoard finds, sickled,
while the ground grumbles.
                           the many
eye openings in it

those: in many times
darkened district.

under cloud hiccup
this:
Murnau-esque chasing,
at top of voice perhaps,
half eyeless,
in opened-up, and
                         again
darkened region:
                Murnau's
                wild shadow-chase.
                                 so
goes the region, so it runs ragged –

under many blank-outs,
and photoflashes.

steadycam, grumbling.

yes.
hmm yes.

there is a progress of the condition
in the grumbling, the insubordinate
organ.
        shadow finding, that
dives into the
channel of hearing. not light-

progredienz, nichts von gegennacht. nein, schatten.
und ziemlich
verschattete gegnd ist das menschenohr.

                    tcha. ja. so

geht, jagend,
unter wolkenschluckauf
die gesichtete, gesichelte

gegnd in fetzn.

progress, nothing of counter-night. no, shadow.
and a rather
shadow-buried region is the human ear.

                  hmm. yes. so

chasing,
under cloud hiccup
the sifted, sickled

region runs ragged.

Amaryllis belladonna L.

doch diese augen leuchten schwarz noch im vergehn.
groß, als ob der garten, ins herbar gepreßt, so einfach
zu begreifen wäre wie ein netz. die äderungssysteme

stehen auf und haben weite: strahl und gift. so rauscht
die blüte, findet sich gedruckt; hat altersfarbe, stockt
und hat das licht um im papier sich selbst zu sehn.

ist dies der druck, den die linné'sche lumen-uhr –
der zeiger reckt den hals –, ist dies ein platzen, regnen,
und verrinnen? ist farben-rast dies, andacht, rasen, köp-

fe – hängen lassen? und hat die eigene farbenskala,
aufgeschäumtes rot, mit festem blick. der stockfleck
nennt die stunde; blitzen. nachtgesicht lädt auf.

Amaryllis belladonna L.

but these eyes gleam black still in withering.
large, as if the garden, pressed into the herbal, were
as easy to understand as a net. the veining systems

stand up and are spacious: glow and poison. so the blossom
rustles, finds itself pressed; has aged colour, halts
and has enough light to see itself in the paper.

is this the specimen, which the Linnæan aperture clock –
the hand stretches its neck out – is this a bursting, raining,
and washing away? is this colour-rest, ceremony, lawn,

heads – letting droop? and has its own colour scale,
foaming up red, with steady gaze. the stem stain
tells the time; flashing. night face charges up.

Sibylle Hellespontica

Alter magnetbänder schweres mahlen.
prophezeiungen aus hingestückter stimme,
verzerrt. fast eine ältre frauenstimme kaum, bei un-

mißverständlichem inhalt –
band schleift; stimmband in auflösung begriffen.
der ihr pelzbesatz; das rote, theure cape.

von den schläfn wehend: tüllschleier – durch tüllschleier
sprache;
   und der pokal steht feste über einem buch.

Sibyl of the Hellespont

Heavy milling of old magnetic tape.
prophesies from chopped up voice,
distorted. almost an older woman's voice hardly, with the

unmistakable content –
tape slips; vocal chords in the process of dissolving.
who has her fur apparel; the red, dear cape.

fluttering from her temples: a tulle veil – through a tulle veil
speech;
       and the goblet stands firmly over a book.

Sibylle Cumaea

Sie ist es:
die macht Aeneas zur schnecke.

sagt ihm,
was zu tun sei – opfern.

sagt's ihm,
dem Aeneas, eindringlich, macht ihn zur sau
mit schauerlicher stimme:

was dem gotte,
was Apollo zusteht.

           wie die codes sind;
pflichten, zukünftiges; wie:
trächtige wölfin,
stadtgründungs-arie,
& daß nichts läuft, hier,
ohne goldnen zweig.

         & zeigt
dem neuankömmling (rolltreppe
im magen)

                  wo's langgeht.

runter.

Cumaean Sibyl

It's her:
who turns Aeneas into a snail.

says to him,
what has to be done – a sacrifice.

says it to him,
to Aeneas, urgently, turns him into a sow
with thrilling voice:

what is due to the god,
to Apollo.

       how the codes are;
duties, of the future; how:
gravid she-wolf,
town-foundation aria.
& that nothing will work, here,
without the golden bough.

       & shows
the newcomer (escalator
in his stomach)

            where the story goes.

downwards.

Notes

RATINGER HOF

Tribal punk club in Düsseldorf. For the scene TK is describing, see the many photos on the Internet. *Steiff*: manufacturer of teddy-bears.

Valeska Gert and *Berber*: 'grotesque' performers of the Weimar era, comparable to punk self-presentation.

CAPTAIN BREHM

sluice: verklappen, a word referring in the public mind to notorious cases of releasing chemical pollution through an outlet pipe (by opening the *klappe* or lid).

Brehm's Tierleben is a very famous 19th-century book on zoology, describing animals which pollution will remove from the picture. Although the poem is a "marine piece" the reference is more to pollution from famous factories entering Germany's internal waterways.

HERMESBABY. AUSPICIUM

Formal well-wish containing the words for birds, looking. The poem is about the Austrian poet Friederike Mayröcker.

OUTSIDE BROADCAST

lehmann: probably Wilhelm Lehmann, poet popular after the war for soothing evocations of the continuity of Nature, but not much read now.

POLAR PICTOGRAM

Translation of the Swedish: *älskling* is "darling". "to be able to work in the cold is a question of concentration (…) I don't think it's difficult (…) I am, besides, studying the Eskimos now, and they probably have it even colder, says Thomas Kling, a Düsseldorfer who is a guest at Vasa" and then: "Dutch stove, side-dish, fireplace, Dutch stove".

PETERSBURG HANGING STYLE

Daniil: probably Daniil Kharms, Russian writer (1905-1942)

DÜSSELDORF CONFIDENTIAL

penck: A.R. Penck (1939-2017), painter of "Palaeolithic" themes who took his name from a famous geologist.

Title refers to the Königsallee, the luxury shopping street in Düsseldorf.

PAVANE IN PENZING

The title holds in some coded and neo-futurist way the sounds of the words "reinhard priessnitz". Priessnitz (1945-1985) was a Viennese avant-garde poet (*vier und vierzig gedichte*) who published little in his lifetime and is in some way an emblem of avant-garde purity and research. Widely regarded as untranslatable. *schreittanz* is basse-danse, a predecessor of the pavane, likewise a stately "walking" dance; *pavane* is used here as it is more familiar.

PUBLIC TRANSPORT

make the holes fly out of the cheese : line from a song (the Blankenese Polo-naise) played at Carnival time.

AVALANCHE LIGHT

Märklin : most recognized brand of model-train makers

GNASH

Oskar Pastior. Pastior was a German-speaking Transylvanian poet, author of *Krimgotische Fächer* (Crimean Gothic Fans). André de Toth was a one-eyed film director and the subject is probably a film by de Toth, in a bad print, featuring the temple of Paestum as scenery.

PORTRAIT JB

'JB' is Joseph Beuys, a hippie performance artist. *Humboldt* : name of an ocean current but also of a secondary school in Düsseldorf.

Friderizianum: original exhibition palace for the *Documenta* exhibitions in Kassel.

dayshade : Nightshade and tomato are both solanums, so tomato could be 'dayshade'.

THE DESTROYED

88 is the age of the speaker when remembering

NECKLACING

Gesang der Jünglinge : choral work by Karlheinz Stockhausen.

serner : Walter Serner (1889-1942), Dada prose-writer from Karlovy Vary (Karlsbad in German). Kling visited Karlovy Vary as a 15-year old, referred to in the poem – the one time the word "I" appears in his poems.

RUMA

Ruma: Etruscan form of 'Roma'.

lined up : Kling had earlier quoted a passage from Theodor Mommsen about the earliest Etruscan writing not being in lines but written in a spiral.

THE COLOURS IN VOGUE 1914

Hoffmann : chief of staff of the entire Eastern Front.

BLACK FOREST

Sander : August Sander, took thousands of photos of ordinary people in the first decade of the 20th century.

Shuffle sequence : people are looking at an album of family photographs but do not look through in chronological order.

Heads of the wise : the lens suddenly slips to New Guinea, mixing in the ethnographical photographs from New Guinea because the forest dwellers are being looked at as primitives.
tusk shell: scaphopoda.

GHOSTS

Eastern New Guinea was a German colony from 1884 until 1919.

PIETER BRUEGEL

'The Alchemist' is a drawing of around 1558 by Pieter Bruegel the Elder. The *headset* is because the poem is like the commentaries you hear on headsets as you go round a museum.

DER SIMILAUN

The Neolithic mummy later known as Ötzi was discovered in a high Alpine valley near the Similaun refuge hut. It had been frozen into the Hauslabjoch glacier since 3000 BC.

Sichtzwang, optic compulsion: refers to a word of Paul Celan's, *Lichtzwang*.

INSTRUCTIONS TO A PAINTER
Calvenschlacht : battle of Chalavaina in 1499.

BEAR SONG
Siberian or North European ethnic groups had a ceremony about the bear hunt which involved keeping the bones of the animal intact and a ritual for its resurrection. The reference is to grief and to silence. The taboo on the real word for 'bear' led to a range of cover-words, used in the ceremony, which may also have been the origin of part of the old European poetic vocabulary. Ostyak: Siberian tribe which tells the bear legends.

AMARYLLIS
Linnæus did propose in 1751 a flower clock where flowers which open at different times of day would tell the time.

SIBYLS
According to legend there were twelve Sibyls. The Cumaean one appears to Aeneas in the *Aeneid* and prophesies the founding of Rome.

SKY DISC OF NEBRA
A disk made from blue copper and gold dated to the middle 2nd millennium BC and showing the heavenly bodies. It is said to be the earliest visual depiction of the cosmos and was illegally dug up in 1999 near the town of Nebra (Saxony). Unjetice-culture.

The cinema theme (Murnau) in 'Epilog' refers obliquely to the miniature camera, endoscopically looking at the poet's lung and its tumour.

Lightning Source UK Ltd.
Milton Keynes UK
UKHW010702011020
370849UK00001B/26